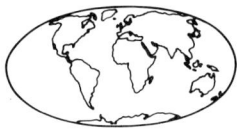

Settlers in the American West

Margaret Killingray

B.T. Batsford Ltd, London

Contents

First published 1988

Typeset by Tek-Art Ltd, Kent
and printed in Great Britain by
Richard Clay Ltd,
Chichester, Sussex
for the publishers
B.T. Batsford Ltd
4 Fitzhardinge Street
London W1H 0AH

ISBN 0 7134 5839 9

Frontispiece
*Migrants with their covered waggon in Loop Valley,
Nebraska, 1886.*

Foreword

Throughout history people have been on the move from one place to another. In this way a large part of the world has become inhabited. For most of human history people moved in small groups, searching for new lands where they could live free from enemies and hunger.

The greatest migration, or movement, of people occurred between 1820 and 1930 and was made possible by the development of the railway and the steam ship. During that period millions of people made the long journey from Europe to America, but also to Australia and New Zealand, and from European Russia eastwards into Siberia. Smaller movements of people also took place in Asia, with Chinese moving into the lands and islands of Southeast Asia and Japanese out into the Pacific and to America.

Most people moved as a result of what can crudely be described as a mixture of "push" and "pull" factors. They were "pushed" out of their homes by poor living conditions, shortage of land, or lack of religious and political freedoms, and "pulled" or attracted to new lands and countries by the hope of a better way of life and new opportunities. For some people migration was largely involuntary: either they did not want to move or they had very little choice. Between 1520 and 1870 millions of Africans were forcibly taken across the Atlantic to America as slaves, and today there are millions of refugees in the world who have been compelled to leave their homes because of war, famine and disease.

Migration mixes people together, not only people from different parts of the same country but also peoples of different languages and cultures. Countries such as the United States and Brazil have been created by people from vastly different backgrounds. And if we look closely at the history of Britain we will see that our language and culture have been shaped by migrants coming to these islands during the last thousand years or more. Migration from Europe to the new lands after 1700 led to the spread of languages (English and Spanish to the Americas, for example), the development of new accents and new cultures, or ways of life.

The aim of this series of books is to look at different examples of "peoples on the move" – why did they leave their original homes? How did they travel? What did they take with them? What did they find in the new lands? How did they settle down? What were relations like between "natives" and newcomers? And what was the impact of new economic systems on the land?

If you have had the experience of moving home, perhaps from one country to another, or even from one place to another *within* a country, then you may be able to share the feelings of people who migrated in the past. If you have never moved home then perhaps these books will help you to understand the reasons why people move, and why in the world today there are, for example, people of European origin living in America and South Africa, and people of African and Asian origin living also in America and in Britain.

The map shows the following labels:

ATLANTIC OCEAN

NEW HAMPSHIRE
MASS
RHODE IS.
CONN
NEW YORK
NEW JERSEY
PENN
DELAWARE
MARYLAND
VIRGINIA
N. CAROLINA
S. CAROLINA
GEORGIA

APPALACHIANS

Forest

Forest

Ohio

Mississippi

Missouri

49th PARALLEL

THE GREAT PLAINS

ROCKY MOUNTAINS

Great Salt Lake

Desert

Desert

WEST

PACIFIC OCEAN

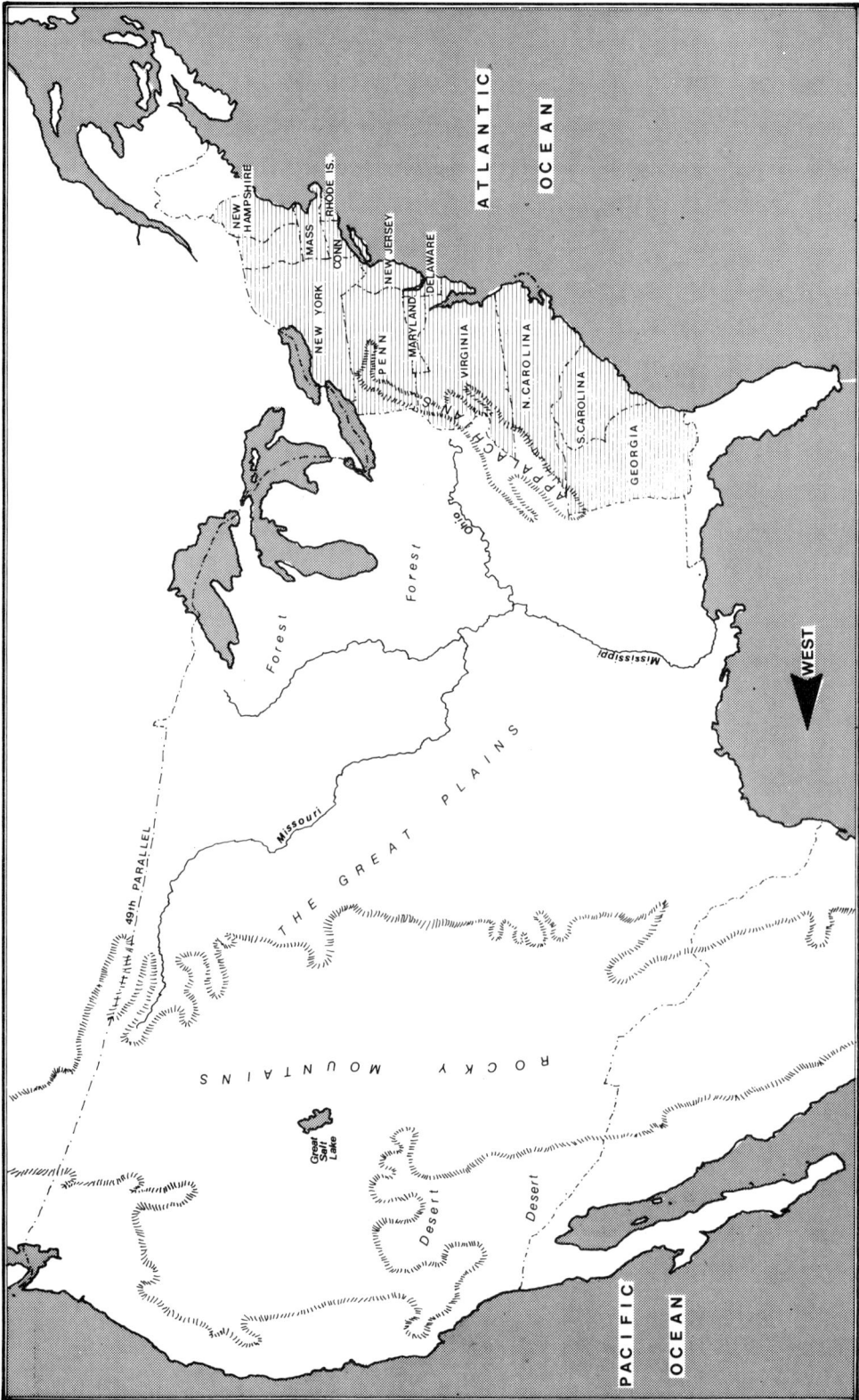

The 13 states and the West, 1790.

1 A Family Moves West: New Jersey to Oregon

Keturah Penton was 15 in 1835 when she started a journal, recording her family history. Her parents, John and Magdalena Penton, lived in New Jersey on the eastern coast of America. They were both born in the United States, but their four parents, Keturah's grandparents, were from England, Sweden, Holland and Ireland. In 1818 John and Magdalena, with their four children, a waggon and a three-horse team, started on their westward travels by moving to Ohio across the Appalachian Mountains. Travelling with two other families, Magdalena and the children boarded a flatboat at Pittsburg and rowed to Cincinnatti, where John Penton met them with the waggon. Sixteen miles from Cincinnatti they bought a 40-acre farm in exchange for one horse, the waggon and $50; ten acres were already cleared and fenced, but the rest was still heavy timber. There were no buildings, but soon they had built a log cabin. The first year the young family worked very hard to feed themselves; father threshed wheat for elderly neighbours in return for part of the crop; he also helped a butcher in return for meat; mother and daughters took in flax to spin and they carded and spun sheep's wool.

Keturah was born in the log cabin in 1820 and remembered moving to a new farm when she was six, where she worked hard, weeding and looking after the cucumber and melon vines and helping to harvest them and get them to market. When she was ten, Keturah began to think about earning her living, since there were now eight in the family. She went to school in the winter, and in the summer, when not working in the fields, earned money looking after the babies of working mothers and washing dishes.

From this home the family moved again in 1835. They went to northern Ohio, to an area of unfarmed forest. Here Keturah met and married George Belknap in 1839, and almost immediately the newly-weds set off for Iowa. Here is her account of the trip, with her own spelling and punctuation:

> On Oct 17th we gathered up our earthly possessions and put them in a two horse wagon and started to find us a home in the far west. We had heard of the prairie land of Illinois but we had never seen anything but heavy timber land, so we set our faces westward [there were no railroads then]. We traveled thru part of Ohio and across Indiana and Illinois and crossed the Mississippi at Fort Madison into Iowa – was four weeks on the way and saw prairie to our hearts content, and

Trees, stumps and rocks made ploughing hard work the first season.

verily we thot the half had never been told.

We camped out every night, took our flour and meat with us and were at home every night, cooked our suppers and slept in our wagon. We had a dutch oven and skilet, tea kettle and coffee pot and when I made bread I made "salt rising".

We stoped at Rushville, Ill. and stayed four weeks, expecting to winter there but we heard of a purchase of land from the Indians west of the Mississippi, and again we hitched up and mid-winter as it was we started never thinking of the danger of being caught on the prairies in a snow storm. . . . Up at 4 oclock in the morning, crossed the river just after noon . . . the next day started as soon as it was light and I had to drive the team again and face the wind, it commenced snowing before we struck the timber. It was hard round snow and it seemed every ball that hit my face would cut to the quick. . . . Oh my but it was cold. The next day we got to the place about noon. . . . The house was a double, hued [hewed] log house, they let us have one room and we unloaded. . . . We made trades with them and got ploughs foder, chickens and hogs.

(Quoted in Cathy Luchetti and Carol Olwell, *Women of the West*, Antelope Island Press, 1982)

Here on the Iowa prairie George had to travel two miles to get timber for fences, but after two years he was able to build a frame house of split and sawn wood. Keturah and George had four children in the eight years they lived in Iowa, but only one survived. Keturah records in her journal the misery and grief of watching her babies and toddler sicken and die. With their surviving son they set out for Oregon in 1848, lured by the tales of gold in California. They travelled by waggon with several other families. When they reached Oregon the men of the party hastily built cabins for their families before leaving for the Californian goldfields. Eventually the men returned, with little to show for their mining adventure, and settled down to farm. The Belknaps had seven more children, four of whom survived, and Keturah herself died in 1913 aged 93.

The Belknaps led an adventurous life, but their story is typical of the many millions of Americans who migrated west during the nineteenth century to start a new life.

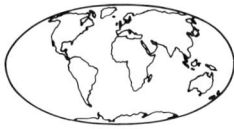

2 The Untouched Continent

The United States in the late twentieth century has a population of 230 million in 50 states, and is the richest and most powerful nation in the world. Two hundred years ago, in 1790, the 13 states from New England to Georgia along the Atlantic coast had a population of four million. The country west of the Mississippi river was virtually empty, except for scattered communities of Indians. This book looks at the years between 1790 and 1890, during which the vast area of continental America was settled, for by 1890 one-third of the 70 million population lived west of the Mississippi.

In the century between 1815 and 1915 around 35 million people migrated to the United States from every part of Europe and beyond. The nineteenth century was a time of upheaval and movement in Europe as well as in America. This upheaval was a part of the economic changes which brought about the rapid expansion of cities and towns, industrial development and population growth. But, with some exceptions, the western United States was opened up and peopled not by European migrants, who went mainly to the cities and settled areas of the East, but by the Americans themselves – the second-, third- and fourth-generation Americans, whose ancestors had arrived there from Britain and north-west Europe in the seventeenth and eighteenth centuries.

There have been many movements of peoples over the centuries, but the westward movement in the nineteenth century of millions of people to settle the great American wilderness has, above all others, caught the imagination of the world. Often fanciful, exaggerated and legendary, "The Western", in film, song and book is part of the cultural heritage of far more people worldwide than the Americans whose story it tells.

A vast, dusty plain, with grotesque cacti standing starkly against a brilliant blue sky. The overland stagecoach, pulled by a team of sweating horses, gallops in a cloud of dust along the rutted trail. Suddenly, down from the scraggy hills swoops an Indian war party, whooping and yelling. The driver cracks his whip, urging the

Outside the saloon: a still from one of John Wayne's many westerns – Rio Bravo.

horses to greater effort – the guard on top of the coach turns, his gun held as steady as the bouncing vehicle will let him...

A dusty, one-street town, with a few shabby buildings. The noise of raucous laughter and the clink of glasses comes from the saloon; outside, listless horses, tied to the rail, flick the flies with their tails. There is the distant whistle of a steam train, the lowing of cattle. Suddenly, a man comes flying through the saloon door and lands in a crumpled heap in the dust of the road...

Again the Indians attack, this time a slow-moving waggon train. The U.S. cavalry, bugles sounding, appears over the horizon and rides to the rescue. The embattled families, crouched within the circle of their waggons, watch as the Indians ride off, leaving their dead braves where the guns of the migrants have brought them down.

Cowboy and Indian, outlaw and sheriff have been part of the folklore of the western world and beyond. *Little House on the Prairie, The Virginian, Paint Your Wagon* and *Calamity Jane* have told the story, albeit a romantic and highly coloured one, of the American West; how a huge continent was peopled, subdued, ploughed and fenced, and covered with roads and cities.

In Europe, population growth led to overcrowded cities and immense pressure on the land. Many areas of Europe could not produce enough food; Norway, for example, mountainous and rocky, just did not have enough fertile land; nor was industrial growth fast enough to support the growing population. But in America there was new, untouched land to spare. So, although American cities grew, and industry and trade expanded, and although millions of immigrants, including many Norwegians, came from overcrowded Europe, there was room for all; room for those who wanted to work on the land, to move west, find their own patch, build a home and start a new life.

In 1783 the 13 states along the Atlantic coast, which had been British colonies, gained their independence. They had fought against King George III's troops in the War of American Independence and had won. A treaty was drawn up and agreed to by both sides, which said that the whole of the area between the Great Lakes and Florida (which was Spanish) west to the Mississippi belonged to the United States. The population of the new republic was mainly of British descent, but also included Dutch, French and Germans, as well as Blacks from Africa, who were slaves in the tobacco- and cotton-growing areas of Virginia and the Carolinas.

Westward from the Atlantic coast were the Appalachian mountains, the first major barrier to migration. Beyond the Appalachians was the mighty Mississippi river, over 500 miles away. Between lay a rich land of forest and rivers, full of wildlife of every kind. To the west of the Mississippi were the Spanish lands of Louisiana; at the mouth of the great river lay the port of New

---

The U.S.A. and the European powers. Texas, the Gadsden Purchase and the territory ceded by Mexico were all previously Spanish areas.

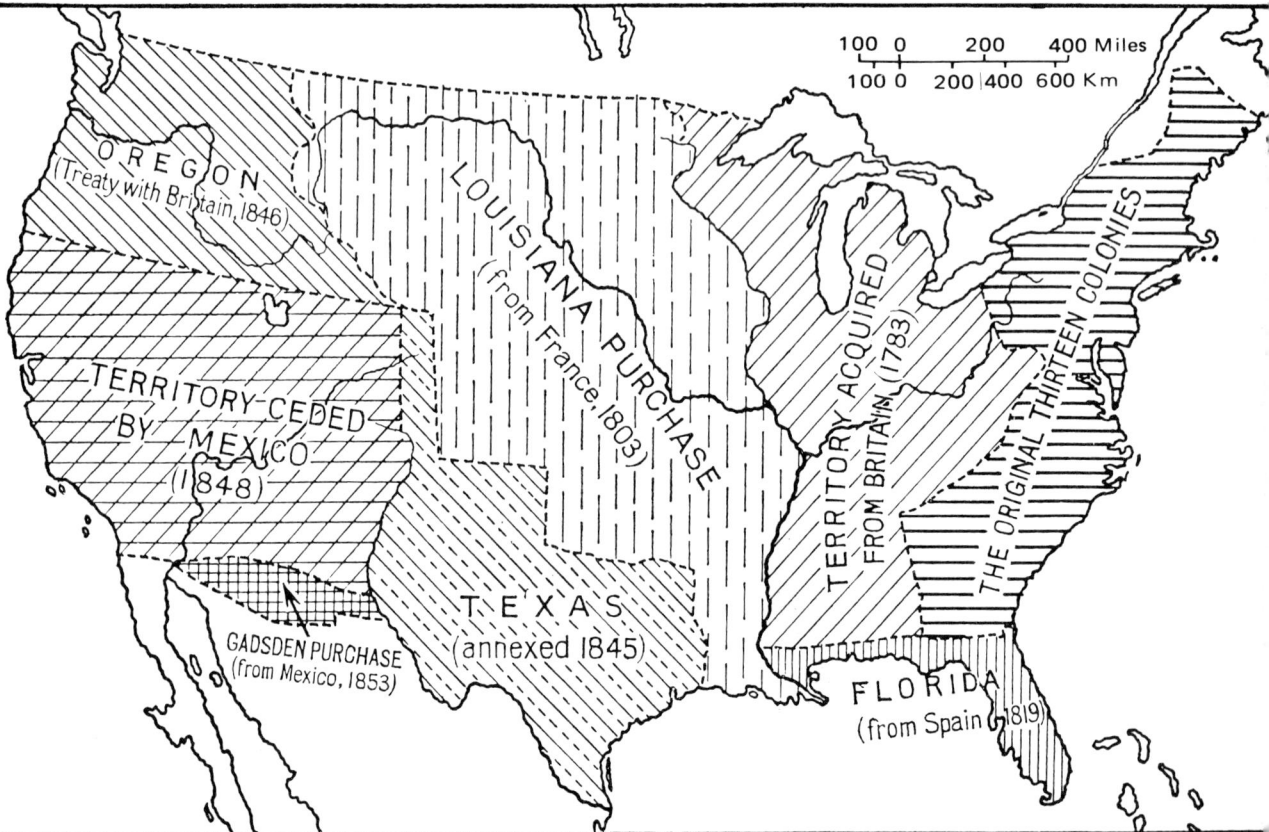

Orleans. To the north of the Great Lakes was British Canada. When the first British settlers arrived in the sixteenth century, the Frontier with the West – that is the imaginary line that divided the settled, farmed land from the forest and the plains – was only a few miles inland. By 1790 this line had reached the Appalachian mountains, and already there were around 100,000 mountain men, trappers, fur traders and explorers beyond the mountains.

What was out there? First there were the forests – birches and pine, elm, oak, sugar maple, walnut and hickory, sycamore and willow – rich in plants and wildlife – bear, moose, deer, wolves, foxes, beavers, geese, ducks, pigeons, birds of every kind and rivers teeming with fish. Then there were the mountains: the Appalachians, rising to 6000 feet (2000 metres), rocky and steep, tangled with dense forest; and the Rockies, the backbone of the continent, a mountain range running from the Arctic in the north to the southern tip of South America, 1000 miles wide in places and sometimes three miles high, cut by ravines and canyons. Between the forests and the Rockies were the Great Plains, 1000 miles of grassland, lush and long in the east where the rainfall was sufficient for farming, short and dry further west where drought was common and the winters fierce. Here were coyotes and wolves, antelope and prairie-dogs, gophers, turkeys and prairie-chickens, and, above all, the great herds of buffalo. In the rain-shadow of the mountains were the deserts, areas of fierce heat and no water, the land of cacti and rattlesnakes; beyond the Rockies lay the wooded, fertile valleys of the Pacific coast. How could four million people clinging to the Atlantic shore take over such a land?

Thomas Jefferson was a Virginian planter brought up on the Frontier and an important

Travellers in the West saw some of the wildest and most rugged scenery in the world.

politician in the federal government set up by the new republic in Washington. He believed strongly that all men had certain basic rights, regardless of their wealth or social class, and had helped to write the famous Declaration of Independence of 1776. He believed that a government should be set up to secure these rights but if the government became undemocratic and took life or liberty away from its people then the people had the right to overthrow it and set up a new government in its place. Such ideas horrified the kings of Britain, France and Spain, all of whom had ruled parts of North America, and even the wealthy merchants of the 13 states felt that Jefferson was too much a supporter of the small farmer. Jefferson had seen the crowded cities, slums and factories of Britain and wanted to encourage a land of small, independent farmers. He wished to make it easy for poor men to take their families west where they could find enough arable land to make a living. But there were those in the government who wanted the land in the West to be priced high enough to prevent easy movement so that there would be plenty of workers for the cities and factories of the East. Jefferson fought his opponents and, in the end, his wishes prevailed.

In 1801, Thomas Jefferson became the third President of the United States. He was committed to encouraging western expansion and was able to make two important contributions towards this.

The area to the west of the Mississippi was called Louisiana – but was much bigger than the state of Louisiana today. In fact, it covered 15 of the present 48 mainland states. Originally colonized by the French in the late seventeenth century, Louisiana had been lost to the Spanish in

> This is perhaps the most famous sentence in the Declaration of Independence, which representatives of the 13 states signed in 1776.
>
> **We hold these truths to be self-evident, that all men are created equal, that they are endowed by their Creator with certain unalienable Rights, that among these are Life, Liberty and the pursuit of Happiness.**

1762, but in 1800 Spain secretly handed it back to France, then ruled by Napoleon. The United States was deeply concerned; Spain had closed the port of New Orleans to American citizens just before the sale, thus making it impossible for them to take their goods down the Mississippi. This was the only trade outlet for large areas of the country, since the overland route to the east coast was still very long and difficult. France was a strong, ambitious country and might make it even more difficult for citizens on the Mississippi frontier. The United States' representative in France began to bargain with Napoleon, hoping at least to buy New Orleans, but Napoleon, who had lost an important battle in the Caribbean, offered the whole of Louisiana; Jefferson jumped at the chance and accepted the new territory for $15 million. "I have bought enough land to satisfy Americans for a thousand years," he said.

Jefferson's second contribution to western expansion was his encouragement of western exploration. He sent two experienced army officers, Lewis and Clark, on an expedition to discover a route to the Pacific. Jefferson thought that the mighty Missouri and Columbia rivers

The Mississippi and its many tributaries formed vital trade routes to the West and South, but they became dangerous obstacles as well to settlers.

both rose in the Rocky Mountains near enough to each other for them to form a continuous route from the East to the West. In fact, Lewis and Clark returned eventually with the news that the Rockies were far higher and wider than anyone had imagined and that many hundreds of miles of almost impassable peaks, gorges and rocky plateaus separated the two rivers. However the rest of their report encouraged people to start on the road west.

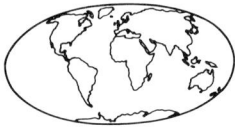

3 The Indian Peoples

This open, rich land of the west, which seemed to the American farmer to be there simply for the taking, was not empty of people. Nor did the early European settlers in New York, Massachusetts, Carolina and Georgia arrive in an uninhabited land. Scattered across the continent in groups of varying size lived the Indian peoples. (They were called "Indians" because when Christopher Columbus first sighted land on his voyage across the Atlantic he thought he had reached India.

These people had as many different languages, cultures and economies as the people of Europe or Asia. As the land and its climate varied, so did the Indians. They saw themselves as separate nations; there were groups in alliance with each other and others who were sworn enemies.

But as the tide of European immigrants slowly occupied the eastern Atlantic coast and began with increasing speed to spread west, so the Indians reluctantly, tragically, fell away before them. They lost all that they valued, until by 1890 they lived beaten and demoralized in small, barren, designated areas called reservations, surrounded by the dynamic, forceful American society which had taken over their land. Basically, it was impossible for the two groups, with their very different cultures, to live together.

Location of some important Indian tribes and the reservations of 1875. By 1890 these reservations had been greatly reduced in size.

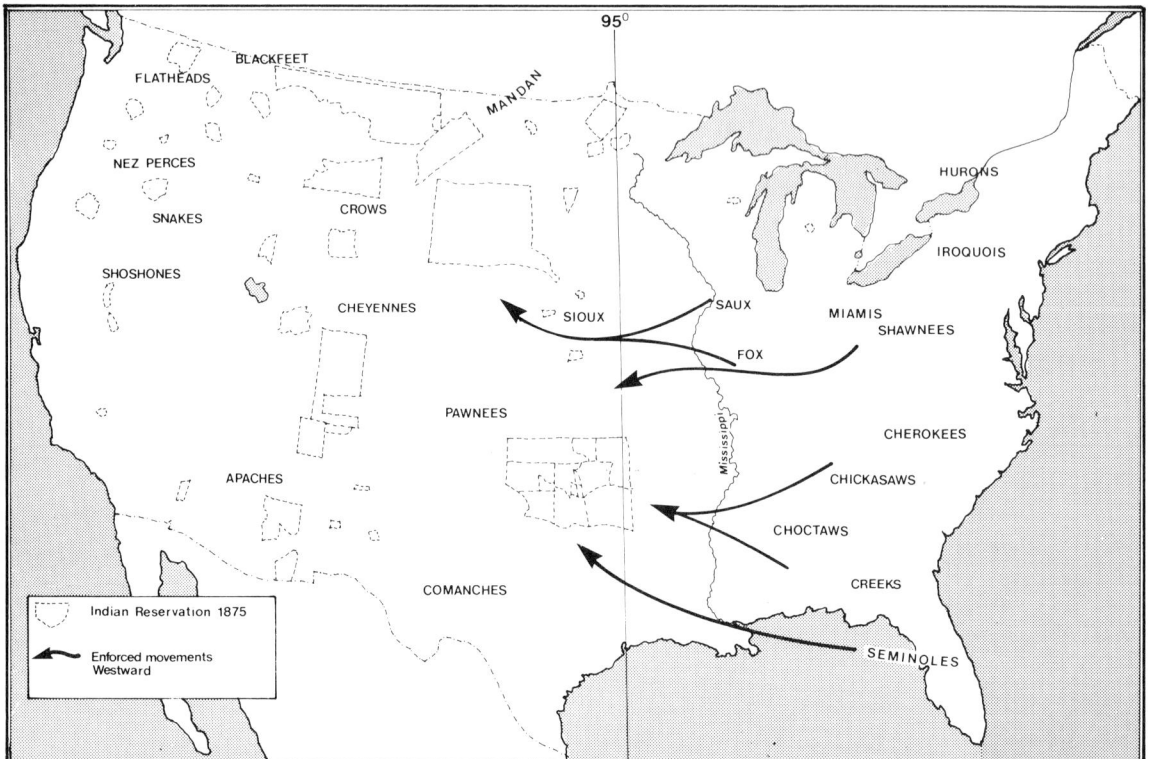

The white Europeans despised and feared the Indians. The Indians were hunters and gatherers, as well as small-scale farmers growing maize and beans. Almost all they needed for food, clothes, shelter, weapons and basic utensils they took from the natural world around them, making little impact on their environment. As they lived in small, scattered groups, there was plenty for all; the small clearings where they grew crops soon reverted to forest or grassland when they moved on. But the white settlers wanted to change the land; to build farmsteads with well-tended, fenced fields; to travel on roads; to raise cows and sheep; and to build towns, churches and prisons. To do this they cut down the trees, ploughed the grasslands, shot wild animals and destroyed their habitat, drained the lakes, and introduced new plants and animals from the "Old World".

During the first 300 years of colonial America the Indians of the eastern coast were steadily dispossessed of their land by treaties they did not understand, and infected by European diseases to which they had no resistance and which decimated and even obliterated whole groups. The scattered remnants were driven west. By 1830 the Wampanoags, Chesapeakes, Potomacs, Hurons, Eries, Mohawks and Senecas, among many others who had inhabited the east coast, had left only their names behind on the map of America. It was then the turn of those Indians who lived to the west of the Appalachians to be overtaken by white settlement and to be cheated out of their lands: the Miamis fought and ceded their lands in Ohio bit by bit until there was none left; the Saux and the Fox fled Illinois.

To the American government there was no solution but to move the Indians out of their lands. They did not farm properly and they wasted the rich resources of the soil which were needed for white civilized settlement. That was how the vast majority of the western migrants saw the problem. Even when Indians were granted by treaty a certain area of land, settlers frequently moved in before government agents or army patrols could stop them, and then the pressure from the settlers to move the Indians on yet again was too great to resist. There were some who thought that the only good Indian was a dead one and advocated a policy of extermination. But as reports came back from explorers of the vast prairie lands of the West that seemed then to be far too barren for farming, the ideal solution seemed to be to move all the Indians on to the Great Plains. No one considered that Indians,

Although many Whites despised and disliked the Indians, there was also a trend that saw them as romantic, but primitive, heroes, as Longfellow did in his famous poem "Hiawatha".

Tecumseh of the Shawnees, tried to unite the Indians of the North-East and the South against the white man. He travelled thousands of miles in the attempt, but failed. He died in battle in 1812. He said:

Where today are the Pequot? Where are the Narragansett, the Mohican, the Pokanoket, and many other once powerful tribes of our people? They have vanished before the avarice and the oppression of the white man, as snow before the summer sun. Will we let ourselves be destroyed in our turn without a struggle, give up our homes, our country bequeathed to us by the Great Spirit, the graves of our dead and everything that is dear and sacred to us? I know you will cry with me "Never! Never!"

used to living in the rich forests and grasslands of the East, would find the plains as inhospitable as the white farmers would do. "I suggest the propriety [suitability] of setting apart an ample

An Ojibway burial ground near the Great Lakes. Sometimes the loss of their ancestral burial places to white development hurt the Indians most, because these sacred sites played an essential part in their rituals and beliefs.

district west of the Mississippi to be guaranteed to the Indian tribes as long as they shall occupy it," said Andrew Jackson, the seventh President of the United States in 1829.

A law was enacted in 1830 which put this idea into effect, setting aside an area in which white people were not allowed to settle. But even before it was passed settlers had moved into Wisconsin and Iowa, so that the "line" had to be moved west from the Mississippi to the 95th meridian.

In the South, the Cherokees, Choktaws, Chickasaws, Creeks and Seminoles had attempted to work their own solution to the problem of living with white Americans. The Cherokees of Georgia, in particular, changed their way of life; they built farmhouses, schools and roads, and fenced their land. They developed a written language and produced a newspaper called the *Cherokee Nation*, which was printed in English and Cherokee. They

Even those in authority thought that there was nothing wrong in taking over Indian lands. The Secretary of the Interior, 1862:

> **The Government has always demanded the removal of the Indians when their lands were required for agricultural purposes by advancing settlements.**

The white agent of the Osage Indians in Kansas, 1864:

> **The Indian lands are the best in the State and justice would demand as well as every consideration of policy and humanity, that these fertile lands should be thrown open to settlement and the abode of civilized and industrious men.**

hoped that by doing so they could stay in Georgia on their lands, becoming part of the state in the same way as their white neighbours. Some of them even owned black slaves, so completely did they identify with the Southern way of life. But their hopes were in vain.

When the Seminoles of Florida were faced with removal to the barren lands of Oklahoma they rose in a war that lasted for nearly ten years. Many runaway slaves fought with them. But when the government of the State of Georgia decided to sieze the lands of the Cherokees for white occupation, the Cherokees took their case to the Supreme Court of the United States. The decision went in their favour, the Court deciding that Georgia had no right to take their lands. But Georgia ignored the ruling, and President Jackson, who disliked Indians, refused to uphold the Court's decision. In 1835 a small proportion of the Cherokees, but none of their leaders, signed a treaty of removal to seven million acres of land in Indian Territory (Oklahoma). In 1838 an American army of 7000 rounded up many thousand Cherokees and force-marched them to Oklahoma through a bitter winter. A quarter of them died on the way; the Cherokees called this their "trail of tears", and when they arrived they found hostile Indians and infertile land.

The interior of a Mandan hut on the Missouri river. Lewis and Clark stayed over winter with the Mandan on their expedition in 1803. Thirty years later, when this engraving was produced, there were only a few Mandan left; the rest had died of smallpox.

No treaty made with the Indians lasted more than a few years, despite the inclusion by the government of promises of permanence – "as long as the stars shall shine and the rivers flow" – and even on the inhospitable plains the Indians were not safe from western expansion. Here, later in the nineteenth century, the Indians' most prolonged resistance was to come.

From *Memorial and Protest of the Cherokee Nation,* 22 June, 1836:

It would be useless to recapitulate [restate] the numerous provisions for the security and protection of the rights of the Cherokees, to be found in the various treaties between their nation and the United States. The Cherokees were happy and prosperous under a scrupulous observance of treaty stipulations by the government of the United States, and from the fostering hand extended over them, they made rapid advances in civilization, morals, and in the arts and sciences. Little did they anticipate, that when taught to think and feel as the American citizen, and to have with him a common interest, they were to be despoiled by their guardian, to become strangers and wanderers in the land of their fathers, forced to return to the savage life, and to seek a new home in the wilds of the far west, and that without their consent. An instrument purporting to be a treaty with the Cherokee people, has recently been made public by the President of the United States, that will have such an operation, if carried into effect. This instrument, . . . [we] aver [say] before the civilized world, and in the presence of Almighty God, is fraudulent, false upon its face, made by unauthorized individuals, without the sanction, and against the wishes, of the great body of the Cherokee people.

4 Crossing the Appalachians

Steadily, throughout the first 30 years or so of the nineteenth century, the rich forests and rivers between the Appalachian mountains and the Mississippi were settled and tamed; trees were cut down, fields cleared for planting and the Indians persuaded by any means to give up their lands and eventually moved to the inhospitable plains further west. When the land became too crowded for the genuine pioneer, and another man's axe could be heard in the forest, he would pack up and move further west. Others, less adventurous, would take over his fields, and communities would build towns with schools and churches. By 1820 ten new states had joined the Union and Ohio, Indiana, Illinois, Kentucky, Tennessee, Alabama and Mississippi completed the area between the mountains and the great river. By 1839 there were over four million people in these new lands, out of a population of 12 million.

The farmers who moved over the Appalachians into the new lands were mainly second- and third-generation Americans. There were some immigrants from Europe – mainly Germans, Scandinavians and the Scotch-Irish (that is, descendants of Scots who had settled in Northern Ireland). In fact, between 1790 and 1820 there was little immigration from Europe. During those years Britain was at war with France and later with the United States. The effect of these

---

Crossing the Appalachians
William Keys left Rockbridge County for Ohio in 1805:

We took our journey from the valley of the Old Dominion in September, A.D. 1805, with a strong team, large wagon and heavy load. We proceeded on our way over the Allegheny mountains, Greenbrier hills, Sewell and Gauley mountains, Kanawha rivers and backwater creeks, often impassable by the rising of the river, and arrived at Point Pleasant, where we crossed the Ohio and left most of our troubles behind us. Our company consisted of two family connections, each of which were subdivided into one or two smaller families; and to give promise of a fair beginning, each of them had an infant specimen of young America to carry on the knee, and numbering twenty-three persons in all, eight of whom were full grown men.

We often had to exert all our united strength and skill to prevent our wagons from upsetting, and had often to double teams in order to ascend the steep mountain sides. None of our company met with any accident, but not so with all the emigrants who preceded us on the same route; we sometimes passed the fragments of broken wagon beds, broken furniture and remnants of broken boxes and other marks of damage by upsetting on the mountain side, where the wagon, team and all had rolled over and over down the steep declivity [downward slope], for some rods, until stopped by the intervention of some trees too stout to be prostrated by the mass of broken fragments. By doubling teams, we could reach the mountain top, but to get safely down again called for other contrivances. One expedient frequently tried was to fasten a pretty stout pine tree to the axletree of the wagon with chains, so as to retard the downward course upon the horses. At the foot of such hills and mountains could be seen sundry such trees that had been dragged down for the purpose above named. We arrived at our Highland home in about eight weeks of constant travel, Sundays excepted. . . .
(Quoted in Gerald McFarland, *A Scattered People: An American Family Moves West*, Pantheon Books, 1985)

wars was to leave a "generation gap", during which the new states were peopled by Americans. Later, European immigration increased enormously, but the basic pattern of society and culture had by then been established by people who had lost their ties with Europe and thought and felt as Americans.

Basically, the pioneers moved directly westward, going to lands with similar climate and soil to the ones they had left. They were pioneers in that they were moving to virgin lands, but they were not pioneers in their methods of farming. They wanted to plant the same crops and rear the same animals as they had in the East. Thus settlers from New England moved westward to the Great Lakes, into Ohio, Indiana and Illinois, and in the South, settlers with their black slaves moved from Virginia, the Carolinas and Georgia southwards and westwards to Florida, Alabama and Mississippi, to grow cotton.

They moved partly because they wanted to leave behind the barren soils of the North-East or the depleted soils of the South, where a single crop of tobacco or cotton drained the goodness from the land. They moved, too, because they wanted to be free again to make their own way in life, in their own world, without interference. For them the growing towns and industry of the East were becoming too much like the oppressive systems that their fathers and grandfathers had left behind in Europe. In the new West all men were equal – that is, all adult white males; and they moved west to assert their individual right to own their own land and run their own affairs.

They moved, too, because life in the East was not always easy. On several occasions there were financial crises, or panics, when small businesses went bankrupt, banks failed and debts and mortgages could not be paid. For small farmers and tradesmen this might mean having to sell all their goods and land to pay their debts. In 1837 there was a particularly bad financial panic and many people went west to start again.

Crossing the rugged, rocky, boulder-strewn Appalachians and trekking through the woods and forests of the West was not easy. Most travelled in waggons along narrow, rough tracks, full of potholes and tree stumps. There were several basic roads, or tracks: the Wilderness Road connected Virginia and Kentucky through the Cumberland Gap; Braddock's Road went up the Potomac valley. In 1818 the federal government saw that there was a desperate need for better roads, not only to maintain communication but to encourage a sense of national unity for such a far-flung people. The first national road was built across the mountains; it was 30 feet (10 metres) wide, paved and drained, and soon small settlements with inns and hotels grew up along it to serve the many waggons that trundled westwards.

Another government project was the building of the Erie canal; this 350-mile-long "ditch" joining the Hudson River and Lake Erie was finished in 1825, providing such a crucial link westwards that the cost of taking one ton of freight from New York City to Buffalo on Lake Erie fell from 20 cents to less than 2 cents. Migrants from the northern New

Flat box waggons like these would float across a river if necessary. The metal hoops and canvas covers were sometimes used to make a tent for the migrants' first home.

In 1801 *The Navigator: Containing Directions for Navigating the Monongahela, Allegheny, Ohio and Mississippi Rivers*, by Zadoc Cramer, was published. It went through 12 editions and was an essential guide for flatboat sailors, as well as providing encouragement to many would-be migrants. Cramer wrote:

No country perhaps in the world . . . [is] better watered with limpid streams and navigable rivers than the United States of America. No people better deserve these advantages, or are better calculated to make proper use of them than her industrious and adventurous citizens; a people worthy of all the advantages that nature and art can give them, a people the more meritorious, because they know how to sustain peace and live independent among the crushing empires, the falling of kings, the slaughter and bloodshed of millions and the tumult and corruption and tyranny of all the world beside.
(Quoted in Richard A. Bartlett, *The New Country: A Social History of the American Frontier 1776-1890*, O.U.P., 1974)

Descending the Tennessee River in the early 1800s.

England states used this route to the West.

Once across the mountains, many continued their journey by water. The headwaters of the Ohio river, joining the Mississippi, which reached the sea at New Orleans, were a gateway to huge areas of the West. The migrant families on reaching the river either bought or made a flatboat, which was rather like a shallow-sided box. They piled their tools and seeds, animals and household goods into it and set off downstream for thousands of miles. It was a dangerous journey; there were rapids and sandbanks which sometimes threw the whole family into the river. When they arrived at their chosen destination they broke up the flatboat and either sold the wood for supplies or carted it inland to use in their first home.

The migrant farmers travelled west with high hopes of clearing and farming their own lands – growing not just enough to feed their families, but a surplus with which to trade – but for some the task of clearing the land was much harder than they had expected. Growing crops meant removing the trees, fencing and ploughing, and this was hard, back-breaking work in the first years. In a study of British immigration to the North-West, it was found that many could not clear their land fast enough to grow sufficient quantities for their own needs. A few managed to clear five acres a year.

The Flatboat Trade

As well as carrying new immigrants to their new farms carved out of the western wilderness, the flatboat continued to be used well into the 1850s, even after steamboats were common, to bring the farm produce from the North down to the wharves and docks of New Orleans. Called "arks", "Kentucky flats", or "broad beams", they were oblong and about 14 feet (4.5 metres) wide if they started above the Ohio Falls at Louisville, which were 15 feet (5 metres) wide, but up to 25 feet (8.5 metres) wide below that. They were 50 feet (16.5 metres) or more long, and could carry up to 100 tons of cargo according to size. Rectangular in shape with flat front and back, and sides high enough to protect the cargo, sometimes with a wooden cabin in the centre, they were powered by one or two pairs of large oars and had a rudder. The journeys were risky, and not only because of the physical dangers; there was also the economic risk of arriving in New Orleans with a cargo that might not sell, because so many

By the 1870s there were many different types of boat on the Mississippi river, but flatboats were still being steered down on the river's current.

had arrived with similar goods to sell at the same time.

Miles Stacey of Marietta described a typical cargo of the 1850s:

> Say about 100 barrels of apples placed near the bottom where it was coolest. . . . About 600 barrels of potatoes in next. On top of the load 100 barrels of flour. In the bow of the boat we left a place to pack the pork (I usually butchered 60 or 70 hogs). We'd take about 20 barrels of beans, 25 of sauerkraut, 10 or 15 of onions, 3 or 4 barrels of buckwheat flour, 15 or 20 dozen brooms. I'd get 8 or 10 dozen buckets over at the bucket factory.

(Quoted in Harry N. Schreiber, "The Ohio-Mississippi Flatboat Trade: Some Reconsiderations" in David M. Ells, ed., *The Frontier in American Development*, Cornell U.P., 1969)

A trapper and his ponies spent months wandering in the mountains and forests.

How did these tens of thousands of people end up in a new state with a governor, a state capital and a legislature? Throughout the history of the United States there has always been tension between the states and the federal government. The states, independent of each other and sometimes rivals, wished to see as little interference in their affairs as possible, yet at the same time they frequently wanted the federal authorities to act on their behalf against other states. After independence from Britain and the acquisition of land to the west, some states laid claim to all the land on their western boundaries. In 1795 the Georgia legislature sold, to speculators, land which it did not own and had no right to sell and which later became part of Alabama and Mississippi. It took some years to sort out all the legal wrangles that this caused.

In 1787 a law was passed by the federal government which drew most of the present boundaries of the eastern states and placed all the territory to the west of them in federal hands. Territories were mapped, and as each one was formed it was placed under a governor elected by Congress. When the total population reached 5000 it would elect its own legislature, or parliament. When the population reached 60,000 it became a state of the Union.

Each territory was surveyed westward – in chunks called ranges; then each range was divided into six-mile squares called townships; each township was divided into 36 smaller sections of one square mile. As each was marked out, the land was sold, on very favourable terms. In 1800 a settler could buy a minimum of a half section for $2 an acre; in 1832 he could buy a quarter section at $1¼ an acre. This process has led to the "straight line" pattern of settlement in

The Axe

The axe was perhaps the most valuable and indispensible tool; it was needed to cut down trees, to trim logs to build a cabin and to make stakes for fences and furniture. The demand for axes was enormous and it was such requirements which often stimulated industry back in the East. Samuel and David Collins had started making axes in Connecticut in 1826, and in 1832 at South Canton, Ohio, they set up a factory with a few machines. They appointed a new foreman called Elisha King Root. Root looked at all the stages of axe-making, and divided them up between expert workmen; he devised ways of speeding up the whole process, such as taking a batch of 100 axe-heads and hanging them on a drum revolving in a furnace so that each would receive the same heat to temper the steel. Without these mass-produced axes, stamped with the Collins trade-mark, it would have been difficult for the pioneers to clear the forests with such speed.

much of central United States. Sometimes settlers moved in before the government surveyors had done their work. This happened in Iowa. A new Act had to be passed to make it possible for those already on the land with farms to buy the legal deeds and title when their area was surveyed.

But it is important to remember that the majority of migrants who went west, especially in the second half of the nineteenth century, settled in towns and not on farms. They were builders, carpenters, wheelwrights, storekeepers, barmen, lawyers and journalists. The daily life and small town patterns of the East were planted in the West.

Before the settlers and farmers moved in, the forests and rivers had already been explored by the first pioneers – the mountainmen, traders and trappers. Some of these men were eccentric wanderers who loved the wilderness away from settled lands, but most of them were trappers who hunted animals for their furs. The fur trade

The effect of straightline surveying is seen in this photograph of the prairies in the 1950s.

The Beaver

The beaver is a harmless, furry rodent which weighs, when full grown, about 40 pounds (18 kg). It is friendly enough to be a pet if caught young. It is a nocturnal animal, living much of its waking life in its underwater lodge. It has webbed feet and a broad, scaly tail, about a foot (30 cm) long, six inches (15 cm) wide and ¾ inch (2 cm) thick, which it uses for steering underwater and for propping itself up when it is cutting down a tree. The beaver has four fearsome, self-sharpening incisors, which can grow to seven inches (18 cm) in length and have to be worn down by constant gnawing. They have been known to chop their way through a six inch (15 cm) tree in five minutes. The beaver tows the trees it fells to the dams in which it constructs its lodge. Here, in the skilfully built home with underground passages and underwater entrances, the beavers pair for life and bring up their litters.

made some people very rich, and businessmen set up companies to finance the hunt for furs, buy them from the trappers and then send them to Europe to be made into fashionable felt hats. Beaver was the most sought-after fur, but otter, fox and mink were also taken.

By 1800 the forests of the East had been hunted so much that there were hardly any fur animals left. So the fur trappers moved further west, following the tracks and paths made by the animals and the Indians, and, in the process, providing a vast amount of information on the geography and climate of these far-distant regions. Each summer a place in the wilderness on the east side of the Rockies was chosen by the fur companies as a meeting place for the traders and trappers. There the furs were exchanged for whiskey, guns and other goods from the East to meet the rather limited needs of the mountainmen. These meetings, or rendez-vous, were like large fairs, where old friends met to exchange news; "The rendez-vous", said one writer, "is one continued scene of drunkenness, gambling, and brawling and fighting, as long as the money of the trappers lasts."

But by the end of the 1830s the fur trade had begun to fail. The beaver had become more difficult to find, but fortunately, before the last ones were hunted to extinction, the beaver hat

Jedediah Smith, born in 1799, was the son of a New England farmer. In 1822 he answered a fur company's advertisement in a newspaper for an "enterprising young man to ascend the Missouri River to its source and there to be employed". He was well educated, knew Latin and frequently quoted from the Bible. He searched and trapped for furs throughout the western mountains, covering a vast area. He discovered South Pass, which was to become a major route through the Rockies, and was the first to reach California from the east in 1826. He was imprisoned by the Mexicans and attacked several times by Indians, losing 10 men in one incident, and 15 men, together with all his skins and goods, in another. He crossed the Great Salt Desert in an amazing feat of endurance. He provided material for the map-makers in far-away Washington. In 1830 he left for the South-West on the Sante Fe Trail (see p.28) and was killed by the Comanches.

had ceased to be fashionable in far-away Europe. Many of the trappers and mountainmen became guides to the increasing number of people crossing the Rockies to reach Oregon and California.

5 The Trail to the Pacific

By 1840 there were 26 states. Apart from Wisconsin in the far north, which became a state in 1848, all the land east of the Mississippi had achieved statehood, as had Louisiana, Arkansas and Missouri across the river. Thus all the areas of forest now had growing populations. There were some farming pioneers who had moved a little further west out of the forests and on to the edge of the grassland, but the plains and prairies seemed impossible to the farmers, who thought that trees and plenty of water were essential for settlement. The Great American Desert, as the explorers called it, seemed suitable only as a place of exile for the Indians.

But if America was going to expand any further west this "desert" would have to be crossed, because the next wave of migration would "jump" the plains and begin to occupy the Pacific coast – the modern States of Oregon and California. But in 1840 the boundary of the United States did not extend to the Pacific. The Spanish colony of Mexico, whose capital was Mexico City, spread far further north than present-day Mexico, and included what are now Texas, New Mexico, Arizona, California, Utah and Nevada. Britain claimed Oregon, Washington and Idaho. The lands of the United States ended on the high, barren plains of the North and on the Red River in the South.

Several European nations had been involved in exploring and settling the western United States. Until Britain defeated France in North America in 1763 and Napoleon sold Louisiana to Thomas Jefferson in 1803, many French traders and trappers had hunted and settled down the Mississippi. New Orleans, still a very French city today, was founded by them in 1718, and there are many French names still on the map of America. Spain had ruled whole areas of the continent since the sixteenth century. Much of South and Central America was Spanish, and at the beginning of the nineteenth century Spanish rule extended north into Texas and California, as well as Florida.

The Spanish method of taking over and running

The Ingalls family lived in Wisconsin in the 1860s. As more people moved into the forests round them and the ring of another man's axe could be heard, their pioneering father led the family south-west by waggon to Indian territory in Oklahoma. Here they lived in a log cabin just south of Independence, Kansas, until the army, protecting the Indian lands from white settlement moved them on. Back across Kansas, Missouri and Iowa, the family settled again in south-west Minnesota, living for a time in a dug-out built into the bank of a creek. Drought, grasshoppers and, finally, scarlet fever, persuaded them to move on again, and the father accepted work with a railroad construction company in order to recoup the family losses. They moved west to South Dakota and finally settled on a homestead on the prairie. There they saw the growth of a small town, and experienced the severe winters of the 1880s.

> **The town was like a sore on the beautiful, wild prairie. Old haystacks and manure piles were rotting around the stables, the backs of the stores' false fronts were rough and ugly. The grass was worn now even from Second Street, and gritty dust blew between the buildings. The town smelled of staleness and dust and smoke and a fatty odour of cooking. A dank smell came from the saloons and a musty sourness from the ground by back doors where the dishwater was thrown out. But after you had been in town a little while you did not smell its smells, and there was some interest in seeing strangers go by.**
> (Laura Ingalls Wilder, *Little Town on the Prairie*, 1941; reprinted Puffin books, 1969)

Little Town on the Prairie is one of six books that Laura wrote about her family's experiences in the American West.

a new territory was to send in an officer with troops together with a Catholic priest. The priest would start a mission, where the local Indians would be persuaded to become Catholic Christians and then be taught to serve the King of Spain and to be loyal workers for their Spanish rulers. Many of the priests who went were brave men who longed to pass on their faith to the Indians. They often went into new territories without the protection of soldiers, or stayed after the soldiers had returned to Mexico. Many were killed by Indians or died in the harsh climate. The missions they founded were named after Christian saints and a look at the map of California and Texas will show how many of these mission names remain; San Antonio, San Francisco, Santa Fe, San Diego, and many others.

For a time it was possible for the Spaniards to cross the Rockies into California from what is now Arizona, and a number of people settled there, but, later, Indians became hostile and effectively prevented the route from being used. California was cut off from the rest of the continent, and for several decades was only reached by trading ships which had sailed from Mexico or from the

---

The Texas Rangers patrolled the borders of independent Texas, fighting both Indians and Mexicans. This picture is by Frederic Remington, a famous painter of the West.

eastern United States and Europe round Cape Horn. The Russians, who owned Alaska, had also established a number of small trading settlements reaching down to California. By 1791 Spain badly needed settlers in order to secure her hold on Louisiana. Very few were willing to come from Spain or Mexico, so the area was opened up to U.S. citizens, provided they were Catholics and swore loyalty to Spain. Many of these came from the Southern states, leaving behind soils exhausted and infertile from growing the one crop – cotton – year after year. They brought with them black slaves to work the cotton plantations, and many more moved in when Louisiana became part of the United States in 1812.

The other European power who owned or claimed land in the West, was Britain. Britain claimed the whole of Oregon, which included the present state of Oregon, as well as the states of Washington and Idaho, and parts of Canada as far north as Russian Alaska. In Oregon there were small trading posts, which were collecting points for the rich harvest of furs that British and American trappers brought to be shipped out to Europe and the eastern United States. Here, too, the Rockies were an almost impenetrable barrier.

In 1819 the federal government signed treaties with both Britain and Spain which began to resolve these territorial disputes. The agreement with Britain recognized the border with British Canada as being the 49th Parallel, although some Americans wanted to fight for the border with Alaska. South of the frontier, the territory of Oregon would be jointly held by Britain and the United States. In the end it would revert to the nation which could colonize it with the greater number of people. Spain agreed to give up all rights to Oregon and to hand over Florida, in return for America giving up all claim to Texas.

Many Americans, especially the large numbers who had settled in Texas, were furious that the federal government had relinquished Texas. However, in 1821 the whole position changed when a liberal government back in Spain decided to withdraw from many of her overseas territories, and Mexico became an independent country. The Mexican government became even more unstable, with different groups vying for power. Governors of outlying territories were never sure who was in charge and sometimes took over themselves, exploiting and harrying the local people.

The Gun

Together with the axe, the gun was an essential item for the western traveller. In the early years of the nineteenth century most carried an American long rifle. These took about a minute to load, gunpowder being measured and poured down the barrel and the ball rammed down with a long rod. When confronting a large grizzly bear, the settler needed to make sure he found his target with his first shot.

Among the German immigrants who came to America in the early years of the century were gunsmiths who began firearm manufacture in Pennsylvania. The most popular rifle they produced was called the Kentucky, a very accurate gun. But this gun was unsuitable for use on horseback and, again, took a long time to load. The need for something different came during the settling of Texas, when the Texas Rangers were fighting both mounted Indians and Mexicans. The Plains Indians were skilful in the use of bows and arrows fired from swift horses. During the minute it took a Texan to reload his rifle the Indian could ride 300 yards and discharge 20 arrows.

The answer to the problem came from a Connecticut man called Samuel Colt, who in 1835, at the age of 21, drew up diagrams for a revolver-action gun and obtained patents for it in Britain and America. He started up the Patent Arms Manufacturing Company of Paterson, New Jersey, and by 1847, after initial failure, was making revolvers for the Mexican

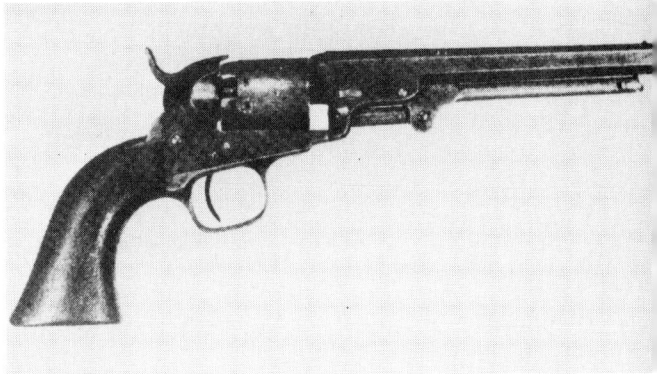

A 36-calibre Colt revolver, 1851 model.

War. This gun had a round chamber with six bullets in it. As one was fired, another moved round ready for the next shot. This gun gave the men fighting on horseback an immense advantage over those with rifles or bows and arrows. Mary Maverick, who lived in San Antonio, Texas, recorded in her diary for 8 June 1844 that John Hays, a Texas Ranger, told her of a battle 12 days earlier in which he and 14 men had been followed by 70 Comanches. She wrote:

Hays modestly gave the credit of the victory to the wonderful marksmanship of every ranger and the total surprise of the Indians caused by the new six-shooters, which they had never seen or heard of before.

Most Americans were convinced that the whole continent south of the 49th Parallel and north of the Rio Grande should be part of the United States. This conviction has been called America's "Manifest Destiny" – her belief that it was obvious that all the land west of the first 13 states as far as the Pacific was *meant* to be part of the Union. In many ways they were right; European powers, with their governments thousands of miles away across the Atlantic, taking decisions for lands they had never seen, were at a huge disadvantage.

With Mexico's trade with Europe coming to an end, the first Americans to take advantage of the disappearance of Spain were traders who took the trail to Sante Fe, where they could sell at a profit a vast range of goods that had become scarce in northern Mexico. Soon the Santa Fe Trail was busy with waggons rolling down from Missouri to the South-West. The Indians of the Plains quite frequently attacked the traders. Treaties were drawn up with the Osages and the Kansas, who promised to leave the waggon trains in peace, but the Comanches remained at war with all intruders.

Meanwhile, the American citizens who lived in Mexican Texas found their lives made increasingly difficult by Mexico's political and military inefficiency and corruption. A report of 1829 showed that of the 25,000 inhabitants 22,000 were U.S. immigrants. This worried the Mexicans, who attempted to impose closer supervision, and by 1835, despite many negotiations, the situation had deteriorated into war between Texans and Mexicans. The Mexican dictator, Santa Anna, fought ruthlessly, but after several victories he became too complacent and the Texans defeated his army and captured him.

For nearly ten years Texas was an independent republic, but political rivalries between the leaders and constant skirmishes with both Indians and Mexicans as well as financial problems led them into the Union, and Texas became a state in 1845, the same year as Florida. But settling the Texas question did not end America's disputes with Mexico. War broke out again, the United States won decisively, and the treaty that ended the war in 1848 made California and what is now Arizona and New Mexico as well as Utah and Nevada, new federal territory.

But even before California became American through the treaty of 1848, pioneers had begun to look for a route across the Rockies to the Pacific. News of the fertile coastal plains trickled east; many would-be emigrants did not wish to move to Texas, which was a Southern, slave-owning state. Keeping as they had always done to lands of similar climate, Northerners turned their eyes to Oregon. The distance and the terrain made waggon journeys to the Pacific coast a daunting undertaking. Previously, pioneers going west had often done the journey in short legs, staying perhaps two or three years in one place before moving on. Now the immense distances across the plains and the mountains had to be done at one go. Attempts were made to extend the Santa Fe Trail through to California, but waggons were never able to get through, and at one point, at the crossing of the Colorado river, pack-horses had to be unloaded and led down man-made stone steps.

Not until 1843 to Oregon and 1844 to California were wheeled vehicles able to cross the huge barrier of the Rockies. The Rev. Marcus Whitman, a medical missionary, led the first waggon train from Independence, Missouri,

The Rocky mountains were an enormous obstacle to waggons and horses. When waggons broke down, or a family was sick, they would sometimes lag far behind the main waggon train.

through South Pass, an unusually wide pass over the Rockies, to the Willamette valley in Oregon. He had already established a mission there, having travelled on horseback in 1836. By 1846 several waggon trains had got through the "1000 miles of desert and 500 miles of mountains, no man in his right mind would think of wandering", as a Missouri newspaper put it. More than 1300 people crossed in 1846 alone. There were disasters; nearly 70 died in 1845 when a group tried a short cut through the Cascade mountains, and one estimate put the number of dead in the years between 1841 and 1861 at 10,000. But as the numbers travelling increased, so the trails became easier to follow; they were sometimes over a mile wide across the prairie. They crossed the Rockies at South Pass and continued to Fort Hall, where the waggon trains divided to take the Oregon or California trail.

For protection they travelled in groups, each one with a leader and outriders. Usually there were oxen – cheaper than mules – to pull the waggons. The journey took about six months, starting in May when the new grass began to grow, so that the animals could feed, and ending in October, so that the last mountain was crossed before the snows of winter. One Californian waggon train was caught in the snow crossing the Sierra mountains. When the rescue parties reached them in the spring many had died and the survivors had had to resort to cannibalism.

The waggon was like a home on wheels: sick and tired, old and very young found a haven inside. In it was carried all that the family needed for six months' travel through a wilderness; flour and cornmeal, bacon and sugar, blankets and clothes, bedding and cutlery, nails and pins, ropes and candles, axes and guns, fiddles and washbowls. The journey involved ferrying the waggons across rivers like the Platte; crossing 60 miles of desert, with all water and fodder having to be carried, and heaving the waggons over the Bear Pass in California and lowering them down by rope. Large numbers arrived by sea, increasingly crossing the Isthmus of Panama overland, rather than sailing the long way around the tip of South America. This route marked the beginning of U.S. involvement in Central America.

Throughout the 1840s a steady stream of migrants crossed into Oregon and California, but in 1848 came a discovery that turned the stream into a flood. Gold was found in the Sacramento valley in the same year that California was ceded by Mexico to the United States. Now there was no barrier to settlement, and in addition there was an incentive that had an overwhelming effect on migration. Men poured into the mountains to find gold. They came by sea and by land. Sailors left their ships, workers their shops and warehouses, soldiers left the forts, and all newspapers in San Francisco ceased publication. By early 1849 some 5000 men had come to the gold rivers and mountains from outside California, but by the end of the year the figure had reached 50,000. California's population grew at a rate that was

---

Miriam Davis was born to a poor family in New York in 1817. She married a teacher and they lived in Montreal, Canada, for 11 years before migrating to Kansas in 1856. She wrote a book about her experiences, called *Went to Kansas*, which was published in 1862.

May 3rd. The women and children, who slept in their wagons last night, got a good drenching from the heavy shower. It was fortunate for mother, sister, myself, and children, that lodgings were found for us in a house. My husband said not a rain drop found him; he had the whole wagon to himself, besides all of our Indian blankets...

"What! fast in the mud, and with our wagon tongue broke?"

"Why yes, to be sure." So a long time is spent before my husband and Dr. House can put our vehicle in moving order again. Meanwhile we women folks and children must sit quietly in the wagon to keep out of the rain – lunch on soda biscuit, look at the deep, black mud in which our wagon is set...

May 11th. "Made" but a few miles yesterday. Forded the Little Osage; the last river, they say, we have to ford... our wagon is heavily loaded ... eight trunks, one valise, three carpet bags, a box of soda crackers, 200 lbs. flour, 100 lbs. corn meal, a few lbs. of sugar, rice, dried apple one washtub of little trees, utensils for cooking, and two provision boxes – say nothing of mother, a good fat sister, self, and two children who ride through the rivers...

(Quoted in Cathy Luchetti with Carol Olwell, *Women of the West*; Antelope Island Press, 1982)

Richard Henry Dana had sailed the Californian coast in the 1830s and had written about his travels in *Two Years Before the Mast*, published in 1840. In the 1869 edition he added an appendix called "Twenty-Four Years After", in which he described his return to San Francisco in 1859. Here is the beginning of this appendix:

It was in the winter of 1835-6 that the ship *Alert*, in the prosecution of her voyage for hides on the remote and almost unknown coast of California, floated into the vast solitude of the Bay of San Francisco. All around was the stillness of nature ... during our whole stay not a sail came or went. Our trade was with remote missions, which sent hides to us in launches manned by their Indians. Our anchorage was between a small island ... and a gravel beach. ... Beyond, to the westward of the landing-place, were dreary sandhills, with little grass to be seen, and few trees, and beyond them higher hills, steep and barren, their sides gullied by the rains. ...

Over a region far beyond our sight there were no other human habitations, except that an enterprising Yankee, years in advance of his time, had put up, on the rising ground above the landing, a shanty of rough boards, where he carried on a very small retail trade between the hide ships and the Indians. ... Not only the neighbourhood of our anchorage, but the entire region of the great bay was a solitude. On the whole coast of California there was not a lighthouse, a beacon, or a buoy. ... Birds swooped and dived about us, wild beasts ranged through the oak groves, and as we slowly floated out of the harbour with the tide, herds of deer came to the water's edge, on the northerly side of the entrance, to gaze at the strange spectacle.

On the evening of Saturday, the 13th of August 1859, the superb steamship *Golden Gate*, gay with crowds of passengers, and lighting the sea for miles around ... neared the entrance to San Francisco, the great centre of a world-wide commerce. Miles out at sea ... gleamed the powerful rays of one of the most costly and effective lighthouses in the world. ... We bore round the point towards the old anchoring-ground of the hide ships, and there, covering the sand-hills and the valleys, stretching from the water's edge to the base of the great hills, flickering all over with the lamps of its streets and houses, lay a city of one hundred thousand inhabitants. Clocks tolled the hour of midnight from its steeples, but the city was alive from the salute of our guns, spreading the news that the fortnightly steamer had come, bringing mails and passengers from the Atlantic world. ...

The dock into which we drew, and the streets about it, were densely crowded with express-wagons and hand-carts to take luggage, coaches and cabs to take passengers; and between one and two o'clock in the morning I found myself comfortably abed in the Oriental Hotel, which stood, as well as I could learn, on the filled-up cove, and not far from the spot where we used to beach our boats from the *Alert*.

Sunday, August 14th. When I awoke in the morning, and looked from my windows over the city of San Francisco, with its storehouses, towers, and steeples; its court-houses, theatres, and hospitals; its daily journals; its well-filled professions; its fortresses and lighthouses; its wharves and harbour, with their thousand-ton clipper ships, more in number than London or Liverpool sheltered that day ... when I looked across the bay to the eastward, and beheld a beautiful town on the fertile, wooded shores ... when I saw all these things, and reflected on what I once saw here, and what now surrounded me, I could scarcely keep my hold on reality at all, or the genuineness of anything, and seemed to myself like one who had moved in "worlds not realised".

Gold miners in California, without their families, often lived crowded together in small huts.

never matched anywhere else in the United States. In 1846 there were only 5000 there (excluding Indians); in 1850 California joined the Union.

Many of the miners discovered little gold, and what they did find they often spent on whiskey and rough entertainment in the boom towns that grew up, sometimes literally, overnight. In many ways this was a different type of migration from those that had happened in the rest of the settled states; it was basically a male migration, and it drew new groups into the country. Cornish miners from England, Italians, Germans, Irish and Chinese came to find gold. In 1858, 300 lonely Italian miners walked nine miles to welcome the first Italian woman to arrive at the mines.

When J.B. Frémont, whose tales of travel in the Far West persuaded many to move there, arrived in San Francisco in 1849 he saw "a few low houses, and many tents [which] covered the base of some of the windswept treeless hills. Deserted ships of all sorts were swinging with the tide." Six years later, San Francisco had 36 newspapers, in French, German, Spanish, Yiddish, Italian and Chinese as well as English. Indeed the city grew too fast, and soon there were signs that certain aspects of life in San Francisco were getting out of control. The wooden shacks, hastily erected, frequently burnt down, but for some time no fire brigade was set up. Men gained and lost large sums of money, giving them to adventurers who convinced them they had found a new gold strike. When the easy gold had been picked and big mining companies began to move in, gangs of penniless men terrorized parts of the city.

This lawlessness and lack of ordinary city government was a feature of many of the boom towns that sprang up where gold and silver were discovered – and there were many further strikes throughout the mountains of the West, particularly in Colorado, Nevada and Montana, Arizona, Idaho and the Dakotas. The mining bonanza increased enormously the population of these Far Western states. Growth which had taken years elsewhere, happened in months. Sometimes the finds were greatly exaggerated, and the disappointed miners moved on to the next strike, leaving shattered valleys and deserted towns. But the traders and builders, farmers and craftsmen followed them, and small towns and settlements with a more balanced lifestyle and less "fever" grew up where the miners had passed through.

During the 1850s and 1860s there was increasing tension and resentment between the Southern, slave-owning states and the Northern, free, states. We have already seen that as the migrants moved west they tended to move inland parallel with their own state of origin, so that they

---

Often those who made money during gold rushes were not the miners but those who provided the services for the miners, like this steamship company in 1861.

stayed in areas of similar climate and soil conditions, and that they took their culture and way of life with them. Southerners, in particular, needed to keep moving on. Tobacco, which had been the first major Southern crop, and then cotton, were grown on single-crop plantations. Unlike farmers in the North, Southerners did not vary their crops from year to year, so the soil never had a chance to replace the nutrients that one type of plant used. In the end, cotton exhausted the soil, and the profits from the crops grew less each year. Rich plantation owners, with slaves, large houses and many servants, had to move on in order to grow sufficient high-yield cotton to earn enough money to keep themselves rich. As they moved into Alabama and Mississippi it was the black slaves who broke the new ground, built cabins and put up fences. When the cotton planters reached Texas they had come to the limit of their westward expansion: further west there was insufficient rainfall to grow cotton.

The South was agricultural and under-developed. Its society was divided into the rich, autocratic planters, who were rulers of little kingdoms, the many very poor Whites and the black slaves. The North was dynamic, urban, industrial, fast growing and saw itself as democratic – a society where no man could assume to rule another. Both North and South resented each other's way of life and were anxious to maintain their numbers in the federal government. So each time western migration led to the creation of a new state, tempers flared and some sort of compromise had to be reached. In 1820, Missouri (a slave state) was admitted to the Union only because Maine (a non-slave state) came in at the same time. There were attempts to work out formulae to decide which states would be slave and which not, but the mistrust was such that none lasted in the long term. Matters came to a head when Kansas and Nebraska, two new territories, were allowed to decide for themselves whether or not they would be slave states. Southerners decided to "win" Kansas by moving in and swamping the territory with pro-South voters. Abolitionist Northerners, who wanted to see the end of slavery in the South, tried to do the same, and for several years bitter fighting took place between the two groups in Kansas. The quarrel deepened and widened, until in 1860 seven Southern states formed the Confederate States of America and left the Union. Civil War followed, for the North, under

President Abraham Lincoln, was determined that the Union should not be divided.

Although the Civil War was caused in part by issues raised by the settlement of the West, the battles were fought in the East, and western migration continued during the war years. By the time the war ended in 1863, Minnesota, Oregon, Kansas and West Virginia had been added to the Union, and the North had succeeded in keeping the Union intact and freeing all the black slaves. For a time, however, life for Southern Blacks was even harder than it had been when they were slaves. There was a great deal of misery and cruelty as economic and social conditions deteriorated and Southern bitterness flared. When federal troops left the South to sort itself out many Blacks left as well, and in 1879 around 80,000 set off for Kansas, walking up the Chisholm Trail or taking boats up the Mississippi. But for them it was going to be very hard. Northern democracy and the great ideals of individual freedom turned out to apply to white men whose origins lay many generations back in North-West Europe. All other groups, and particularly the Blacks, found suspicion and intolerance wherever they went.

6 The Prairie

Lieutenant Zebulon Montgomery Pike, who led several expeditions across the plains between 1805 and 1807, wrote extensive reports and journals which while greatly encouraging migration westwards as far as the Mississippi and Missouri rivers also strengthened the belief that the High Plains were "a desert" fit only for Indians.

> From these immense prairies may arise one great advantage to the United States, viz; the restriction of our population to some certain limits, and thereby a continuation of the Union. Our citizens being so prone to rambling and extending themselves on the frontiers will, through necessity, be constrained to limit their extent on the west to the borders of the Missouri and Mississippi, while they leave the prairies incapable of cultivation to the wandering uncivilized aborigines of the country.

(Quoted in Elliot Cover, *The Expeditions of Zebulon Montgomery Pike*, New York, 1895; in Walter Prescott Webb, *The Great Plains*, Grosset & Dunlap, 1931)

Major Stephen Long, a traveller to the West in 1819, confirmed this unfavourable impression of the Great Plains:

> I do not hesitate in giving the opinion that it is almost wholly unfit for cultivation and, of course, uninhabitable by a people depending upon agriculture for their substance.... The scarcity of wood and water will prove an insuperable obstacle in the way of settling the country.

(Quoted in Thwaites, Reubens and Gold, eds., *Edwin James's Account of an Expedition from Pittsburg to the Rocky Mountains, Performed in the Years 1819-1820 under the Command of Major S. Long*, Cleveland 1904-7; in Webb, *The Great Plains*)

Now the only large area left unfarmed and under-populated was the plains and prairies of mid-America. This area had been called the Great American Desert, and the farmer pioneers from the East were convinced that the best land was the forested and well-watered lands that covered the eastern United States. However, pressure on these lands led an increasing number to move out onto the eastern plains, firstly to the river valleys and creeks, and then up on to the grasslands themselves. Here, sometimes to their surprise, they found richly fertile soil, adequate rainfall, and, once they had ploughed the matted grass-roots, or sod, they were rewarded with a far easier task than those struggling with tree clearance to the east.

But there still remained the huge, almost waterless and treeless western prairie. Settlement here would require not only new techniques but also a solution to the problem of the increasingly harrassed, desperate and antagonistic Indian peoples. Of the 300,000 Indians left in 1865 more than two-thirds lived on the Great Plains.

But there was another obstacle to settlement on the plains for farmers, and that was the buffalo. Of all the wild animals which made the prairies their home, the most impressive must have been the buffalo, or bison. Huge, shaggy animals, sometimes 6 feet (2 metres) tall at the shoulders, they roamed in vast herds, grazing on the endless plains and moving with the seasons. Sometimes they walked in single file, using the same deeply worn tracks, hundreds of miles long. Herds could cover tens of square miles. Numbers have been estimated at 40-50 million in the 1830s.

They were easy prey for the Plains Indians on horseback, and they provided almost all their needs: meat, fresh and dried; thick hides for winter coats and bedcovers; and tanned hides for clothes, moccasins, the tents in which they lived, the boats in which they crossed the rivers, and

Ploughing the matted sod of the prairie defeated the farmers until stronger ploughs were manufactured.

Artist and writer George Catlin travelled throughout the West in the 1830s and 1850s, recording and painting what he saw; here the Sioux Indians hunt buffalo.

the shields which warded off arrows and lances. Buffalo bones were used for tools, hoes, axes and needles; the sinews were made into thread; boiling the hoofs produced a strong glue for arrows; the bladder would carry water; and the dung made good fuel. The very small number of buffalo that the Indians killed made no difference at all to the huge herds. The Indians were nomads, following the herds and carrying all their goods, including their buffalo-hide tents, on the backs of ponies or pulling them along on stretchers made of wood and hide.

As the movement west of white settlers crossed the paths of the migrating buffalo the destruction of the herds began. The building of the railroads across the continent brought the greatest destruction. The construction crews and the miners slaughtered them in thousands. They were hunted – sometimes for their hides, sometimes just for sport and sometimes as a deliberate policy to starve the Indians. Rotting carcases were left where the animals had been killed. The bleached bones were used to mark hundreds of miles of waggon track. During the 1860s and 1870s the last herds were exterminated, and by 1890 there were probably only 1000 or so buffalo left. William Cody, "Buffalo Bill", was employed to supply meat to a construction company building a railroad, and he alone killed 4000 animals in a year and a half.

With the end of the buffalo, the Indian tribes of the plains could no longer support themselves. Many died of disease and starvation. Despite heroic attempts to stave off the end of their way of life, once the buffalo had gone there was no hope for the Sioux, the Cheyennes, the Pawnees and the Blackfeet, and they had to accept the restriction of the reservations.

By 1850 there were settlements all over the United States. Following the miners, the farmers and traders had established themselves in every river valley – in fact, everywhere where there was sufficient water. But few had yet attempted to move out on to the high prairies or the desert lands between the mountain ranges in the West. One group, however, had settled in one of these barren and inhospitable regions.

In the 1830s Joseph Smith founded a new religion – the Mormons, or the Church of Jesus Christ of Latter Day Saints, as it is now known. The church held a mixture of Jewish and Christian beliefs with several additions, which, according to Mormon belief, were contained in holy books that had been discovered and translated by Joseph Smith. From the start the church grew rapidly, and also from the start was seen as a threat by the rest of society. The Mormons were a close-knit community who accepted without question the authority of their leaders. Persecution drove the "Saints" to move to a site where they could build their own town, excluding all "gentile" outsiders, and this they did in Illinois. But even here they were not left alone, and in 1844 Joseph Smith was killed by a mob. Their new leader, Brigham Young, was an exceptional man of immense energy and organizing ability. He decided that the Mormons needed to move as far as possible from the United States, and he led a migration across the Mississippi and the plains, over the first range of the Rockies to the Great Salt Lake Desert over 1500 miles away in Mexican territory. Young organized the trek with military discipline and planning, and continued to work with authority and inspired, but dictatorial, leadership after the first 5000 or so believers arrived. The centre of the Mormon community was Salt Lake City.

The Mormons soon realized that there was not enough rain to farm in the way they had done in the East, but their communal patterns of work and central planning meant that they were able to grow crops by irrigation, using the streams that flowed down from the Wasatch mountains. Gradually the community increased in numbers as many further church members came to Zion, as they called Salt Lake City, including migrants who had been converted in Europe by Mormon missionaries.

A Mormon camp on the plain in the 1850s. While a handcart is repaired, supper is cooked.

Priscilla Merriman was born in Pembroke, Wales in 1835, the second daughter in a family of eight. Her mother died when she was 16 and Priscilla took care of her brothers and sisters. At 17 she became a member of the Church of Jesus Christ of Latter Day Saints, having heard Mormon elders from America preach at a cottage meeting in Tenby. At 21, Priscilla married a young Welsh Mormon elder, Thomas Evans, who had lost his leg at the age of nine while working in a forge as an iron-roller. A month after their marriage the Evans, with other Welsh Mormons, sailed for "Zion", Salt Lake City, Utah.

They took a tug from Pembroke to Liverpool where they boarded a ship for Boston, arriving on 23 May 1856 after a five-week voyage. Priscilla, pregnant, was sick all the way. From Boston they travelled in cattle-cars the 300 miles to Iowa City, where they stayed for three weeks while they and the other migrants had handcarts made.

The first stage of their walk across America was the 300 miles to winter quarters on the Missouri river. Then the 300 Welsh Saints walked on another 1000 miles, with a handcart per family and mule teams to haul tents and surplus flour. The journey was very hard, although not disastrous as it was for later groups who were caught by winter blizzards. They soon ran out of the coffee and bacon they had brought with them and all they had left was flour, with which they were able to bake a little cake. On one occasion they ran out of flour and had to wash out the flour sacks to make gravy.

Many were left in wayside graves, as Priscilla recorded in her journals:

> **Strong men would help the weaker ones, until they themselves were worn out, and some died from the struggle and want of food, and were buried along the wayside. It was heart rending for parents to move on and leave their loved ones to such a fate, as they were so helpless, and had no material for coffins. Children and young folks too, had to move on and leave father or mother or both.**

Thomas, with his wooden leg, had particular problems:

> **My husband, in walking from twenty to twenty-five miles per day [had pain] where the knee rested on the pad: the friction caused it to gather and break and was most painful. But he had to endure it or remain behind.**

After nearly four months travelling on foot:

> **We reached Salt Lake City on October 2nd 1856, tired weary with bleeding feet, our clothing worn out and so weak we were nearly starved, but thankful to our Heavenly Father for bringing us to Zion.**
> **(Quoted in Cathy Luchetti with Carol Olwell, *Women of the West*, Antelope Island Press, 1982)**

But, unlike other territories, the Mormon lands did not become a state of the Union until 1896. The Mormons were different from other western migrants, in that they did not want to be American, and for years many hoped that they could form an independent state, as Texas was for ten years. For a time there was an explosive situation, in which non-Mormon U.S. forces confronted the Mormons. There was some violence on both sides, but eventually the Mormons realized that they could not win such a fight and accepted federal control. They had to abandon their policy of allowing men to have more than one wife, and the U.S. authorities appointed a Mormon governor.

The Mormons had shown that it was possible to settle in the barren lands, but not all areas were close enough to mountain streams to make use of them for irrigation, nor did any other group in this land of rugged individualism have the kind of authoritarian political organization that would make such communal activities possible.

The next group to move on to the prairies did not come from the East, but from the South. Neither horses nor domestic cattle were native to America. The Spaniards had brought both with them in the sixteenth century. Much of the desert of northern Mexico was grazed by herds of small, bony cattle called Texas Longhorns; they provided little beef or milk, but they were hardy.

The end of the trail; stock yards at a railhead, where the cattle await a train for the East.

When the Mexicans left, the Texans took over the cattle of the plains. There were no fences – with no timber to speak of, it was not possible to fence the ranches. This led to the practice of branding cattle with the owner's mark and letting them roam free on the open range.

Many Texans fought for the South during the Civil War and when they returned, like the rest of the defeated South, they had no money and few resources. But the herds, left to themselves, had grazed and grown. Then rumours of a beef shortage in the fast-expanding cities of the North-East spread to the South. There had already been some trading of beef cattle, by ship from New Orleans and even overland to the California gold-mining centres, but the huge distances to the markets of the North-East made such a trade impracticable until, in the 1860s, the railroads began to reach across the continent.

The coming of the railroads changed western migration in very significant ways. Distances shrank; home and family were never so far away again, and it was even possible to return East. The first railroad that crossed the entire continent was completed in 1869, when two companies – Union Pacific and Central Pacific, one coming from the East and the other from the West – met at Promontory Point in Utah. For the cattlemen it meant that the herds could be driven north over the open ranges, roaming and grazing, finding fodder and water at no cost to the drover, and increasing in number – or at least replacing losses – as calves were born on the way. When they came to the railhead they were loaded on to cattle-trucks for eastern markets. For 20 years cowboys worked the herds north to Abilene,

Sedalia and to Dodge City, boom towns that grew up at the railheads in the same haphazard and hasty way that the mining towns had. They travelled the Chisholm Trail, and the Goodnight-Loving Trail, named after the first men who had used them. Out of this dirty, boring, dangerous work somehow grew the legend of the western cowboy.

For a time the profits from the beef trade were good enough to encourage many to accumulate huge herds of cattle. They were dependent on the vast, open, grassy plains where the herds could graze widely enough always to find fresh food. Where there was farmland and fenced fields, clashes, sometimes violent, occurred between the farmers and the cattle owners. But it was the climate that defeated the cattle herders in the end. By the mid-1880s the plains of Montana, Dakota and Nebraska were over-stocked and overgrazed. The drought summers of 1885 and 1886 left the plains dry and parched. The huge herds were already weak when two really bad winters struck. The temperature plunged to well below freezing, and blizzards drove the cattle southwards on to the barbed wire fences that now were beginning to string out across the plains. When the spring of 1887 came 80 per cent of the million head of cattle in Montana were dead. The melting snow revealed piles of dead beasts. Perhaps the buffalo had had their revenge. That was the end of the open range – cattle herds after that were far smaller and were kept in fenced areas so that they could be moved to new grass in a planned way – and with the cattle gone the way was open for the farming of the High Plains.

Sarah Winnemucca, born in 1844, was a Paiute Indian from Nevada. She became a translator for the United States army and worked hard to help her people. She wrote a book, *Life among the Piutes: Their Wrongs and Claims*, published in 1883, to publicize all the injustices they had suffered. The spelling of Piutes has been changed to Paiutes since Sarah wrote. Here she describes the Pyramid Lake reservation, given to the Paiutes in 1860, which she recalls as being "sixty miles long and fifteen wide".

The line is where the railroad now crosses the river, and it takes in two beautiful lakes, one called Pyramid Lake, and the one on the eastern side, Muddy Lake. We Piutes have always lived there on the river. . . .
Since the railroad ran through in 1867, the white people have taken all the best parts of the reservation from us, and one of the Lakes, also.
The first work that my people did on the reservation was to dig a ditch, to put up a grist-mill and a saw-mill . . . but the saw-mill and the grist-mill were never seen or heard of by my people, though the printed report in the United States Statutes, which my husband found lately in the Boston Athenaeum, says twenty-five thousand dollars was appropriated to build them. Where did it go? The report says these mills were sold for the benefit of the Indians who were to be paid in lumber for houses, but no stick of lumber have they ever received. My people do not own any timber land now. The white people are using the ditch which my people made to irrigate their land. This is the way we are treated by our white brothers. Is it that the government is cheated by its own agents who make these reports?
In 1865 we had . . . trouble with our white brothers. It was early in the spring, and we were then living at Dayton, Nevada, when a company of soldiers came through the place and stopped and spoke to some of my people and said, "You have been stealing cattle from the white people." They said also that they would kill everything that came in their way, men, women and children. . . . These soldiers had gone only sixty miles away . . . rode up to [my people's] encampment, and fired into it and killed almost all the people that were there. Oh, it is a fearful thing to tell, but it must be told. . . . I had one baby brother killed there. . . . Yet my people kept peaceful. . .
(Quoted in Cathy Luchetti with Carol Olwell, *Women of the West*, Antelope Island Press, 1982)

But in the 1830s the Plains had been designated the home of the Indian. Over the years since then, by treaties that were constantly broken and by military action, the white man had taken over more and more of the land that he had previously given to the tribes. The railroads were granted federal land enabling them to build right across Indian lands, and the miners and prospectors totally ignored Indian land rights where the possibility of riches in gold and silver lay – and after such areas were settled the government dispossessed the Indians and moved them out. The end of the buffalo took the Indians' livelihood away and made them dependent on government hand-outs from government-employed Indian agents, who were frequently tough, unscrupulous and exploitive men.

In 1851 Thomas Fitzpatrick, a trapper and one of the few sympathetic Indian agents, who worked on the Platte river, was so concerned about the slaughter of the buffalo and the effects of new diseases on the Indians that he called a meeting between the government and the tribes at Fort Laramie. He feared that war was imminent, and because of his good relationship with them, many of the Indians came, despite their suspicion of the government. The Sioux, Cheyennes, Arapahos, Crows and Assiniboines agreed to a policy of concentration, whereby as separate nations they should be settled on certain areas of land that "once defined would be theirs for all time". Article 3 of this treaty said "The United States bind themselves to protect the Indian nations against all depredations [robbery] by the people of the United States." This proved to be a tragically empty promise. In fact, by agreeing to settle on separate areas the Indians had made it easier for their lands to be whittled away and misappropriated, because they were now divided from each other.

In the 1880s the Sioux, defeated and broken – in battle, by crop failure, by the end of the buffalo, and by epidemics of measles – lived on their reservation at Pine Ridge, South Dakota, and prayed:

> **Father have pity on us**
> **We are crying for thirst**
> **All is gone.**
> **The buffalo are gone**
> **They are all gone**
> **Take pity on us, Father**
> **We are dancing as you wished**
> **Because you commanded us.**
> **We dance hard**
> **We dance long**
> **Hear us and help us**
> **Take away the white man**
> **Send back the buffalo.**

As they prayed, they danced the Ghost Dance with a fervour of longing, hoping that their faith might restore their lost way of life in a way that practical measures had failed to do. Nervous

Sioux Indians perform a Ghost Dance, painted by Remington.

agents on the reservation mistrusted this upsurge of religious excitement and sent for the army, and in 1890, at Wounded Knee, soldiers massacred 200 unarmed Sioux – men, women and children – in the last "battle" of the century-long conflict.

Some of the groups were more prepared to resist the white encroachments than others. Young warrior bands of Sioux, Comanches and Cheyennes continued to attack railroad construction workers, waggon trains and even the army. Most white settlers regarded the land as theirs by right and the Indians as something less than human; they misunderstood and feared the Indians and fed their fear on stories of massacres and atrocities. But ferocity and brutality were not only Indian characteristics. In 1864, for example, an army colonel led the Colorado militia in an attack on a village of Cheyenne Indians, killing 500 men, women and children in an indiscriminate and savage way.

The Sioux fought on and off throughout the 1860s and 1870s. In 1876 they wiped out a force of over 200 men under General George Custer. But this was a brief triumph. They were forced to surrender and to concede yet more land, being restricted to a small reservation. The Apaches suffered the same relentless pursuit by the army in the South, sometimes winning a skirmish, sometimes gaining some ground. But all the Indian wars of the 1870s – the Red River War, the

Sioux War, the Nez Perce Wars, the Ute war and the legendary Geronimo's final act of rebellion in which he led a group of Apaches into a Mexican mountain retreat – were acts of rebellion against the reservation system and the hopelessness of the Indians' situation.

The Apaches finally surrendered on the basis of the army's promise that they would be allowed to return to their home in Arizona after two years' exile. But this promise was not kept, and they were shipped out to Florida and after two years to Oklahoma, including not just Geronimo and his rebels, but also those who had stayed quietly on the reservation and those who had actively helped the army quell the uprising that had led to these savage terms.

The Indians were defeated and dispossessed. The final act of misguided government intervention came in 1887 when, in order to break up the tightly knit tribal relationships, which the government saw as the greatest threat to peace, an Act was passed allowing individual Indians to own land in the reservation, rather than the tribe as a whole. Once again, the speculators and land grabbers moved in, cheating and defrauding the

The Sioux encamped near Fort Laramie, which is on the extreme left of the picture.

Indians, who lost yet more of their land.

Slowly, throughout the 1870s and 1880s the farmers who had dared to attempt the farming of the high western plains discovered the techniques which led to the huge wheat crops of the 1890s onwards. But they had to change the way they farmed, and this was something few western migrants had been prepared to do.

The main problems were lack of water, lack of wood for fencing material and the fact that no crops they had previously grown could survive the drought and the cold. They learnt to plough after every fall of rain or snow to prevent evaporation, and to leave some land fallow every year. They used wind pumps to raise the water from the very deep wells that were dug. The invention of barbed wire meant that they could at last protect their crops from domestic and wild animals. Finally, in the 1880s, migrants brought with them new strains of hard winter wheat from Turkey which could survive both the drought of summer and the frosts of winter.

In the Introduction to the Census of 1890 were these words:

> **Up to and including 1880 the country had a frontier of settlement, but at present the unsettled area has been so broken into by isolated bodies of settlement that there can hardly be said to be a frontier line.**

The West had been tamed; there was no longer a frontier – Montana, North and South Dakota, Washington, Idaho and Wyoming all became

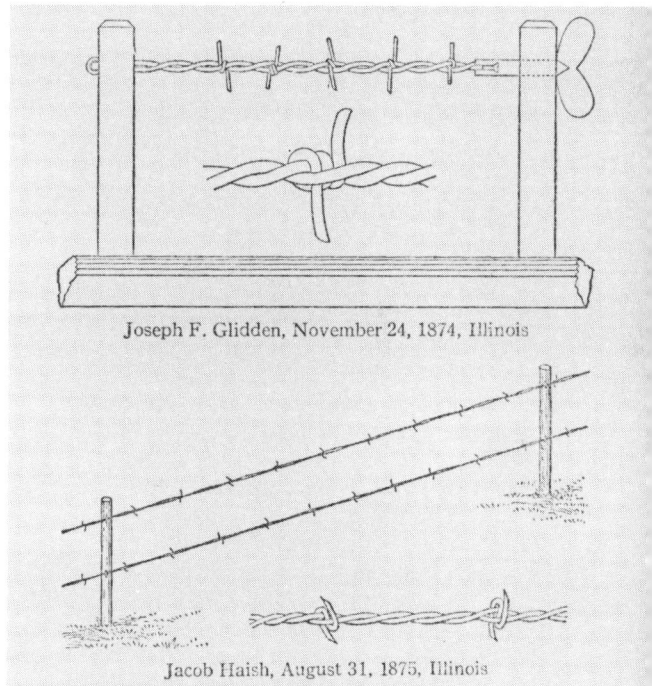

Joseph F. Glidden, November 24, 1874, Illinois

Jacob Haish, August 31, 1875, Illinois

Of the many varieties of wire fencing, these two became the most successful.

states in 1889 and 1890. Of course, such a huge continent still contained many wild areas, and migrants continued to move from state to state, but the railroads, towns, stations, ranches and farms formed a basic network covering the whole of continental America.

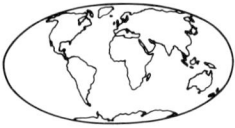

7 Building a New Life

At the end of their journey the first pioneers found themselves on a patch of untouched forest or open grassland, with their waggon and horses or oxen and some basic domestic and farming equipment. Here they had to construct a home, feed themselves, and eventually build up a community, a city and a state.

The first task was to build a home to live in. Except in areas where timber was scarce or unsuitable, this would usually be a log cabin. The farmer selected, cut down and trimmed sufficient similarly sized trunks or branches, which he would then pile one on top of each other, notching or jointing the corners, to form a small, rectangular house. There would be a door with leather hinges and a leather latch to open it. The floor was of beaten, flattened earth, or logs cut in half, rounded side down. The cabin would have a chimney, made of dried mud and stone, which served the fireplace or cast-iron stove. The fierce winters of the continent had to be taken seriously, and a good source of heat and enough fuel for the

A log cabin in Idaho in the 1880s.

A dug-out in Nebraska in the 1890s. In the winter snows, only the chimney would be visible.

Mrs Alice Blackwell Baldwin married an officer in the Thirty-Seventh Infantry at her parents' house in Detroit in December 1867. He was stationed at Fort Harker, Kansas, and he took her there straight away. The journey was long, cold and monotonous – from Detroit to Junction City by train, then by ox-drawn freight waggon. Their home was a dug-out on the flat, bleak, snow-covered plain. She later wrote her husband's biography, *Memoirs of the Late Frank D. Baldwin, Major General U.S.A.*, published in 1929. Here she recalls her first marital home:

I gazed with disgusted disappointment around the bare, squalid room. Its conveniences were limited to one camp chair, two empty candle boxes and a huge box stove, red with rust and grime, its hearth gone and the space filled with a tobacco-stained hill of ashes, the peak of which was surrounded by "chewed-out [tobacco] quids" of unknown vintage. . . . The walls of the kitchen were stayed and supported by logs, while the ceiling was of the same material and covered with dirt. Canvas covered the ceiling and dirt sides. It sagged slightly in the center and trembled under the scampering feet of pack-rats and prairie mice.

(Quoted in Richard A. Bartlett, *The New Country: A Social History of the American Frontier, 1776-1890*, O.U.P., 1974)

winter were matters of life or death. For this reason the logs, once in place, had to be caulked with mud and straw to keep the wind and snow out of the cracks.

But sometimes there was not enough wood to build a cabin. Some settlers lived in dug-outs – rooms carved out of the hillside, with perhaps the canvas from the waggon strung up for a ceiling to prevent the dirt, leaves and insects in the roof from falling on those inside. The front might be made from what wood was available, or from woven branches plastered in mud, or with sod bricks – brick-shaped blocks of prairie grass roots cut like turf from the ground. On the flat plains of Nebraska and the Dakotas, often the whole house would be made from these sods.

As an area became more settled, so the pioneers extended their homes, adding attics to the log cabins or abandoning them to their horses and building a house of new, sawn timber from the local saw mill, with glass windows. For, on average, within five years of initial settlement

A sod house in Dakota in the 1880s.

there were more "bought" timber or even brick houses than cabins, and the basics of a small town had begun to take shape. The furniture inside the cabins would be very basic at first, but many took with them one or two precious pieces of furniture or ornaments – a writing desk or some plate or cup – that reminded them of their home back east. As the months went by, in his spare time the farmer would make a rocking chair, or a bed for a growing child who till then had been sleeping on the floor by the stove. Once or twice a year the waggon would be hitched, and the 10-, 20- or more mile journey to the local store in town would provide material for dresses, a book or some new tin mugs, as well as sugar, white flour, and even candy.

Until the first crops were harvested the family depended on the beans, flour, salt and corn they had carried with them, as well as on the game and fish that they could hunt and catch. "Kitchen garden" vegetables would be added to the diet and, later, goods brought from the store. But in most ways the family, especially in the earlier years of the nineteenth century, had to be self-supporting, making the furniture, weaving cloth from their sheeps' wool, making their mattresses from straw or dried grasses, making soap and candles, and providing their own entertainment.

It may sound cosy and adventurous, exciting and rewarding, but the success of such a pioneering way of life depended not only on the weather and the skill of individual members of the family, but almost above all else on their health. An accident with a heavy log while building a cabin, a badly broken leg, and the family's chances of a successful future could be finished. Apart from accidents with guns and axes, the people of the West suffered from all the usual infectious diseases of childhood, as well as from malaria, tetanus, typhoid and other water- and insect-borne diseases.

As in Europe, the development of medical science lagged far behind all other developments during the industrial revolution, so that the pioneers' distance from the doctors and hospitals of the East was not always a disadvantage. Diseases and infections spread with fatal rapidity in the crowded hospitals and cities of the East, but were kept at bay in the West by the lack of contact between widely scattered farming families. Infant mortality fell, particularly in western regions, during the nineteenth century, and with early marriage and large families the population increased at a very fast rate. Pioneer recipe books for those years are filled with concoctions to ward off common illnesses, poultices for broken bones and treatment for real and imagined ills. Some were learnt from the Indian herbal doctors; some probably worked; others had little goodness in them, except to give the patient confidence that someone was doing something practical to make him or her better.

Some of the worst health problems were met on the migrant waggon trains travelling to Oregon and California: deficiency diseases caused by the scanty basic supplies; epidemics which spread in the close quarters of the waggons; diseases caused by contaminated water supplies; coupled with the sheer exhaustion as the waggon leaders harrassed and pushed to reach the West before supplies ran out, snow blocked mountain passes or Indian attacks weakened the oxen.

In many ways it was the women who bore the brunt of these tragedies. Bearing children, sometimes without even the comfort and aid of another woman, watching over the life-threatening or fatal illness of perhaps several children, the women must have rejoiced as neighbours moved in, small towns grew up, a general store and a school were opened and church services started. In these ways the difficulties and loneliness of pioneer farming were softened.

Many families were sustained through their early years in the West by a strong, individual, Christian faith. Travelling preachers, usually from Baptist or Methodist church traditions, went from community to community on the frontier, meeting in a cabin and boosting the faith of the migrants. As communities grew, a small church was built by local subscription and the fellowship would build up. These churches were independent and democratic, with no sense of hierarchy outside the community. Sometimes a local farmer with more than usual Bible knowledge would be appointed minister. Gradually, associations of churches grew up, most of which were Baptist or Methodist. It was many years before the less adaptable hierarchies of the Catholic and Episcopalian Churches established themselves beyond the Appalachians.

Schools, too, were considered an essential part of a civilized society, and a system that could educate children throughout the scattered communities of the new territories grew up. A

Trying to maintain home life in a waggon was not easy, as Charlotte Pengra, crossing to California in the 1840s, recorded:

During the hours her party traveled, Charlotte Pengra walked beside the wagons, driving the cattle and gathering buffalo chips. At night she cooked, baked bread for the next noon meal, and washed clothes. Three successive summer days illustrate how trying these small chores could be. Her train pulled out early on a Monday morning, only to be halted by rain and a flash flood; Mrs. Pengra washed and dried her family's wet clothes in the afternoon while doing her daily baking. On Tuesday the wagons pushed hard to make up for lost time, forcing her to trot all day to keep up. In camp that night there was no time to rest. Before going to bed, she wrote, "Kept busy in preparing tea and doing other things preparatory for the morrow. I baked a cracker pudding, warm biscuits and made tea, and after supper stewed two pans of dried apples, and made two loaves of bread, got my work done up, beds made, and child asleep, and have written in my journal. Pretty tired of course." The same routine devoured the next day and evening: "I have done a washing. Stewed apples, made pies and baked a rice pudding, and mended our wagon cover. Rather tired." And the next: "baked biscuits, stewed berries, fried meat, boiled and mashed potatoes, and made tea for supper, afterward baked bread. Thus you see I have not much rest."

(Quoted in J. Faragher and C. Stansell, "Women and Their Families on the Overland Trail to California and Oregon, 1842-1867", L. Dinnerstein and K.T. Jackson, eds., *American Vistas, 1607-1877*, O.U.P., 1987)

simple building with a few desks and a stove was erected, and some local farmers and tradesmen would get together, appoint a school board to run the school, select and appoint a school teacher and from time to time check that discipline and progress were as they should be. In the early days some teachers travelled from group to group, providing each with about two months of schooling, the children being expected to work on their family farms for the rest of the year. By

Where there was no wood for fuel, dried buffalo dung, or chips, were collected. This picture shows just how flat and featureless the plains were.

1850 every state had a school fund, and taxes were used to maintain common schools in every community. Although some people complained at the imposition of such taxes and wished to be able to educate their children privately, most were convinced that the new states in a fast-growing republic needed a unified school system to encourage national identity and patriotism. Gradually, statewide systems of teacher certification were established and also statewide systems of graded materials for use in the schools.

As the small town grew, someone usually started a local newspaper. It would include a little national news that came by train in newspapers from the East or by telegraph. But most of the news was extremely parochial, and sometimes, when the paper was dominated or owned by some sectional interest – cattle ranchers, for example, or a mining company – then even the local news would not be very balanced or independent.

One beloved Methodist circuit rider was the Reverend Wesley Van Orsdel, who arrived at the Blackfoot reservation in northern Montana in June 1872, a fledging parson from Pennsylvania. He had a good voice and had earned his passage on a Missouri river steamboat by singing hymns. The Blackfeet dubbed him "Great Heart" because he was so warm, sympathetic and understanding to them; white settlers, who took to him with equal affection, called him "Brother Van". After a year the young Methodist concluded that the Whites needed religion more than the Indians. Before he died he had established more than 100 Methodist churches in Montana.
(Richard A. Bartlett, *The New Country: A Social History of the American Frontier, 1776-1890*, O.U.P., 1974)

DEPARTMENT OF EDUCATION

DAKOTA COUNTY OF KINGSBURY

Teacher's Certificate

This is to certify that *Miss Laura Ingalls* has been examined by me and found competent to give instruction in *Reading, Orthography, Writing, Arithmetic, Geography, English Grammar, and History* and having exhibited satisfactory testimonials of Good Moral Character, is authorized by this

Third Grade Certificate.

to teach those branches in any common school in the country for the term of twelve months.

Dated this *24th* day of December, *1882*

Geo. A. Williams,
Supt. of Schools,
Kingsbury county, D.T.

Result of examination:

Reading, 62, Writing, 75, History, 98, English Grammar, 81, Arithmetic, 80, Geography, 85

15-year-old Laura Ingall's teaching certificate.

Communication remained a problem throughout the nineteenth century. The federal government invested in various ways to keep people in touch with each other. The railroads had made a huge difference to the transport of both goods and people, cutting the time it took to travel the vast distances. They were the key factor in the growth of cattle ranching and in the settlement of the plains and prairies, but in 1860 there was still ten times the mileage of railroad east of the Mississippi as there was west, and many communities well into the 1880s and 1890s were still so far from a railhead that they needed horse-drawn vehicles for their everyday lives. Stagecoaches were still being manufactured in 1890.

Initially, stagecoaches, carrying freight and passengers, and steamships on the thousands of miles of navigable rivers were run by individuals or small companies; but as the need for coordination became greater, larger companies were set up, or grew out of the smaller ones, to run integrated systems. The Oregon Steam Navigation Company had dominated river transport in the Pacific North-West from 1860, but was eventually bought up by the Northern Pacific Railroad Company. This pattern was followed all over the West, and many famous companies like Wells-Fargo came into being.

There were many colourful stagecoach drivers, with names like Sage Brush Bill, and Charlie Parkhurst. (The latter, rough and profane, chewing tobacco and bullying the passengers, when he died turned out to be a woman!) But it was the large companies that were awarded the Post Office contracts to carry the mail across America. Jim Bunch, who started by running many of the stages in California, called his company "The Telegraph Line of the United States Mail Coaches" and ran from Sacramento to

William Holmes McGuffey was Professor of Ancient Languages at Miami University in Ohio. In 1837 he published a series of readers which he had compiled to teach spelling, enunciation and grammar, and to provide interesting reading matter for a new society almost without books. It is estimated that 122 million copies were sold between 1837 and 1920, and they played an immeasurable part in unifying the nation. There were six graded readers. The themes were typically Victorian, patriotic and moralistic, with a strong emphasis on the value of hard work.

> Work, work, my boy, be not afraid;
> Look labor boldly in the face;
> Take up the hammer or the spade,
> And blush not for your humble place.
>
> There's glory in the shuttle's song;
> There's triumph in the anvil's stroke;
> There's merit in the brave and strong,
> Who dig the mine or fell the oak.

(*McGuffey's Fifth Eclectic Reader*, Signet, New York, 1962)

Rough and Ready and Nevada City in 1851. In 1857 he took over the Post Office contract between San Diego, California, and San Antonio, Texas, across 1500 miles of desert and Apache country. The journey took 30 days. Speed was always the important criterion, and a final attempt to cut the time it took to communicate between East and West was the Pony Express. This lasted for just a year and a half; the riders cut the journey from Missouri to California to 10 days, but they could not carry nearly enough mail and the system was far too costly. It ended as the transcontinental telegraph line was completed.

Law and order, policing and punishment and a system of courts of law took time to be established in the West. Small, scattered communities of farming families often had little need for such things, hoping that the army would be available if Indians got out of hand and threatened war and bloodshed. But the small towns that sprang up in mining areas, or where there were important railheads for cattle – Dodge City and Virginia City for example – had more than their fair share of lawlessness, violence and gangs of outlaws who made life uncomfortable for more law-abiding citizens. In some places respectable

The United States army was never a strong presence in the West. It was used mainly to patrol the boundaries between America and Mexico, and those between areas of white and Indian settlement, to keep Indians on the reservations and Whites out – although, on the whole, the army units were more zealous in chasing the Indians back than preventing Whites moving in. Forts were built by the army at points on the boundaries and along the trails. Some of the forts had small settlements round them which grew into towns, like Fort Worth and Fort Laramie. Others were later abandoned. Some acted as trading posts. Bents Fort, in Colorado was built by a private individual as a place of rest and protection for the traders on the Santa Fe Trail.

citizens would form vigilante groups and, taking the law into their own hands, would deal themselves with those they saw as law-breakers. This was rough-and-ready justice, and no doubt there were tragic mistakes. In Virginia City, Montana, in 1863, for example, vigilantes hanged

Wells-Fargo overland mail leaving San Francisco for the East in 1858.

20 of the worst criminals in the space of six weeks.

Many of these problems – providing law and order, doctors and medical care, schools and colleges, postal services and goods for sale – arose firstly because the distances involved were so great and the available means of transport were so slow (before the development of the railroads nothing could travel faster than a horse), and, secondly, because the West was populated and developed at such a fast rate. Sometimes only ten years elapsed between arrival of the first pioneers and the emergence of a fully fledged state with governor and legislature. But, basically, the system worked, and by 1890 the continental United States was complete – Utah, the Mormon State was admitted to the Union in 1896; Oklahoma, which had been Indian territory, in 1907; and the desert states of Arizona and New Mexico in 1912. The population of the U.S.A. had grown from four million in 1790 to 31 million in 1860 and to 76 million by 1900.

Civilization: a birthday party and a two-storey sawn-timber house. Minnesota in 1900.

James Bryce visited Bismarck, the Dakota territorial capital, in 1883 and recorded his findings in *The American Commonwealth*, published in 1888.

I happened to be at the city of Bismarck in Dakota when this young settlement was laying the corner-stone of its Capitol, intended to contain the halls of the legislature and other State offices of Dakota when that flourishing Territory becomes, as it soon must, a State, or perhaps, for they talk of dividing it, two States. The town was then only some five years old, and may have had six or seven thousand inhabitants. It was gaily decorated for the occasion, and had collected many distinguished guests – General U.S. Grant, several governors of neighbouring States and Territories, railroad potentates, and others. By far the most remarkable figure was that of Sitting Bull, the famous Sioux chief, who had surprised and slain a detachment of the American army some seven years before.

Among the speeches made, in one of which it was proved that as Bismarck was the centre of Dakota, Dakota the centre of the United States, and the United States the centre of the world, Bismarck was destined to be 'the metropolitan hearth of the world's civilization'. However, the feature of the ceremonial which struck us Europeans most was the spot chosen for the Capitol. It was not in the city, nor even on the skirts of the city; it was nearly a mile off, on the top of a hill in the brown and dusty prairie. "Why here?" we asked. . . . "Because the Capitol is intended to be in the centre of the city; it is in this direction that the city is to grow" [was the optimistic answer].

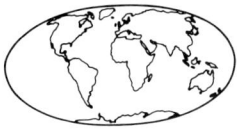

8 The Land

It is difficult for Europeans who live in heavily settled, small-scale states, many of which are smaller in area than a single state of the Union, to realize just how vast the immense American wilderness was. The Alps are dwarfed in comparison with the majestic length and width of the Rockies and only the steppes of Asian Russia can compete with the Great Plains. Most of Europe's forests had been cleared long before the first settlers arrived on the shores of the New World to face thousands of miles of woodland. In Europe there had never been such large areas of unclaimed land. English law assumed all land was legally controlled. One of the great achievements of the federal government was to ensure that all this free, public land was surveyed, divided up and sold in such a way that there was opportunity for small farmers to obtain land in a systematic and orderly way.

The Ordinance of 1785 set out the way in which the land was to be divided, and further Acts controlled its sale and occupation. In 1841 the terms of sale were made more favourable for smaller farmers, and in 1862 the Homestead Act gave settlers land provided they lived on it and farmed it adequately. But these Acts often did not work in the way the government intended. The claims were not always made by independent small farmers setting up home, but were sometimes taken over by speculators, who by fraud and double-dealing acquired areas of land which were then sold to richer farmers for a profit. There was also a great deal of squatting – claim-jumping – where those who thought they had acquired a farm legally found someone else had taken it over in their absence. There was little that could be done. In California, where land grants had been issued by the Mexican government, doubts about the continuing validity of these grants when California became American led to a great deal of harrassment and squatting by land-hungry and gold-hungry men, and some very shady double-dealing by lawyers.

But some of the biggest gains in land rights were made by the railroad companies. They were given huge grants of public land which stretched away each side of the planned route of the track. Landlords acquired large numbers of homesteads by claiming them through false names or through employees, and then were able to obtain the land for themselves by paying small sums per acre to the government or to railroad companies after a year or so – a process which was orginally intended to create small farms owned by single families.

Even by the end of the nineteenth century an adequate solution had still not been found to the problems of framing legislation that would ensure that the huge areas of land would be properly farmed and not misappropriated by large company speculators. An 1877 law to encourage the settlement of arid, irrigable land was exploited by cattle barons to acquire huge areas of prairie for grazing, which they had no intention of irrigating. A Timber Act was passed, which made 160 acres available to a homesteader provided he planted a quarter of it with trees, but, in fact, nearly all the land that had enough water to grow trees had already been sold. Another Timber Act, in 1878, offering 160 acres of timber in California, Nevada, Oregon and Washington for $2 an acre, was simply exploited by the timber companies, who sometimes acquired one 160-acre site, put up their mill, and then stole the timber from the public lands round them, processing and selling it without any thought to restocking the area they pillaged. The federal government had an immense task in controlling the ownership of so much land, and large numbers of individual farmers were able to acquire their homestead at reasonable rates, but far too many large speculators and companies became rich by buying and selling land at prices ordinary farmers could not afford, and many politicians were bribed into turning a blind eye to what was going on.

The farming of the West meant, initially, the clearing and ploughing of lands that had not been farmed before. This presented the pioneer farmers with some special problems – clearing

A steam-driven saw mill, in a forest of Californian pines in the 1860s.

trees and tree stumps, ploughing matted grass – and sometimes the process took several years. The first crops grown were usually corn, squash and beans – Indian crops – that would grow in the inadequately cleared soil. But once the ground had been cleared the settlers, as we have seen, expected to farm in the same way they had done in the East. They had brought with them their eastern crops and animals – swine, sheep, small, wiry cattle, horses and oxen – and these were nurtured as before. But they soon found many of the tools and techniques they had also brought with them inadequate to cope with their new surroundings. The matted grassland of the eastern prairie forced the development of stronger ploughs, for example, and once they had cleared the land the farmers found that they were limited in what they could harvest by the amount of physical work they and their families could do. In a widely scattered community of self-

employed farmers there were few men available to be hired as extra labour. It was possible to plant and harvest only a certain amount of land in a certain length of time, and this pressure led to the development of agricultural machinery which would speed up all the farm processes and allow one man to produce far more crops.

At first this development happened slowly. Farmers cling to the old ways of doing things more than most people; they run the risk of starving if they lose their crops through costly mistakes. Nor could many small homesteaders afford the cost of big agricultural machines. Even when new gadgets did come on the market they were sometimes of limited help in that they speeded up only one step of the process. Harvesting wheat, in particular, presented problems for the farmer with only the traditional scythe and sickle at his disposal. Cyrus McCormick was a Virginian farmer who first

A McCormick "reaper and binder", pushed by a team of horses, around 1900.

solved the problem commercially by inventing and manufacturing a mechanical reaper. Operated by two men this machine could do the work of five or more labourers. Now the farmer had to learn to care for the machinery: the reaper needed oiling and sharpening regularly. Other machines followed – corn planters, horse rakes, cornstalk cutters, threshing machines, combined reapers and harvesters, and mowers.

But farming always remained a risky business and western farmers often had to face hazards that could bring ruin. The fierce climate of the mid-continental landmass was hard to endure for those who had come from the sea-tempered lands of the East: fierce winters which could last for six months, with blizzards that blocked the railroads for months on end; temperatures so low that the breath of cattle and horses froze over their nostrils and suffocated them; hot summers with tornadoes, and wild thunderstorms with hail and rain that could flatten all the crops in a matter of minutes. In Kansas, for example, no rain fell from January 1859 until November 1860. If the farmer had mortgaged his farm, or sold his crops

in advance to buy a new plough or a sewing machine for his wife, he might be bankrupted – forced to sell everything and move on. Some years saw plagues of grasshoppers which ate everything in their path. Fire, too, was a hazard. Sometimes started deliberately to clear land, there were many forest and prairie fires. Some, like the Michigan fire of 1871, caused many deaths and hundreds of square miles of destruction.

The farming settlement of America meant that much of the original natural cover and the wildlife and plants it sustained were destroyed. The beaver and buffalo were just two of the many species that almost completely disappeared. Even the seemingly limitless forests could not withstand the ever-increasing demand for fuel for fires and wood for homes and furniture, for boats and trains, for sidewalks and railroad ties. Wooden trestles, like giant toy constructions, carried trains across rivers, and the locomotives and the steamboats all burnt wood as fuel. Timber barons grew rich, and the lumberjack, like the cowboy, became a figure of American folklore.

Not until 1891 was any attempt made to save the remaining forests from man's decimation.

Rich as America was in all types of wildlife, it was her amazing variety and number of birds that caused most comment from early explorers. Huge flocks of migratory birds – geese, swan and duck – filled the sky in the spring and autumn. There were parrots and humming birds, sea birds and prairie birds – so many that it never occurred to anyone in the nineteenth century that there was any danger of them disappearing. But steadily and wantonly, with guns and traps, their numbers were reduced. Some species became extinct; the last great auk was killed in 1844, the Labrador duck in New York in 1878, the New England heath hen had disappeared by 1931 and the beautiful Carolina parakeet was last seen in Florida in 1912. But perhaps the most amazing loss was the passenger pigeon, a beautiful bird that had existed in huge numbers. Flocks a mile wide and several layers deep were recorded. It has been estimated that there might have been nearly four billion of them in the mid-nineteenth century. It became a popular sport to kill them,

men vying to see how many they could bag. They became a popular delicacy on rich people's dinner tables. The last wild pigeon was killed in 1899, before conservation movements began. Like the buffalo before, it seemed a total impossibility that such huge numbers could be so reduced in less than 30 years.

The ecological changes brought about by the migrants were not entirely destructive, however. Horses, oxen, sheep, cattle, dogs and cats had been introduced by the European settlers, and they soon mingled with the native species. But these were deliberate imports. Others found their way unsuspected. Early colonists brought stores of seed and grain to feed the animals on board ship, and, with them, grasses and weeds native to Europe, thistles and plaintain (which the Indians called European foot). The European honey bee came, as did the house sparrow and the starling.

European migration changed the ecology of America for ever, and only in the twentieth century are people beginning to understand that the constantly changing but delicately balanced

Wooden bridges took huge quantities of wood to build. Here the Union Pacific railroad crosses a creek in Wyoming.

A once productive farm in Colorado abandoned in the 1930s, as dust storms, caused by drought and over-use, overwhelm it.

relationship of tree and grass, insect and bird, air, water and climate is far more important to the health of the whole planet than had ever been imagined. The dustbowls of the South in the 1930s, the smog and atmospheric pollution of cities like Los Angeles, the ruined mining valleys of California, the polluted lakes of Illinois and Wisconsin are the legacy of 200 years of thoughtless, exuberant exploitation. Now, as financial interests are involving the United States in the destruction of the Brazilian forests to the south – which appears to be affecting the migratory patterns of certain birds, which is, in turn, leading to an increase in crop-destructive insects – the question is, can the lessons of the past be learnt to advantage as we move into the twenty-first century?

9 The Legacy

Some of the aspects of the westward settlement of the United States are easy to understand and explain. Because there was room to expand, the population growth of the nineteenth century did not lead to mass emigration as it did in Europe. Americans had somewhere to go when the towns and farmlands became overcrowded. Also, there was land enough to grow the extra food that was needed by the increasing population. The wheat and cattle lands of the West began to produce more just as steam power came to take, by rail and river, the western farmers' surpluses to the markets of the coasts – surpluses that were also exported to Europe and other parts of the world.

But other aspects of the westward movement are more complicated. One American historian, Frederick Jackson Turner, wrote in 1893, that the "frontier" – the idea that there was always new land to occupy to the west – shaped the kind of country that America was in the nineteenth century, and that when the frontier had gone and there were no new lands America would develop in a different way. By the end of the century it was no longer a new, always young, country, but a growing industrial power with an involvement in the outside world, and even with territorial ambitions overseas. Other countries of the world also had their frontiers: Russians moved east across their huge continent into Siberia and Central Asia; Argentinians moved out on to the Pampas; white South Africans moved north. In all of these movements there was the desire for a fresh start, for a new life on new land, and a callous disregard for the peoples who, like the Indians, already inhabited the areas they chose.

Another factor in the settlement of the West that has had an effect on the later history of the United States is the pattern of settlement by peoples from

Modern state boundaries, giving the year each state joined the Union.

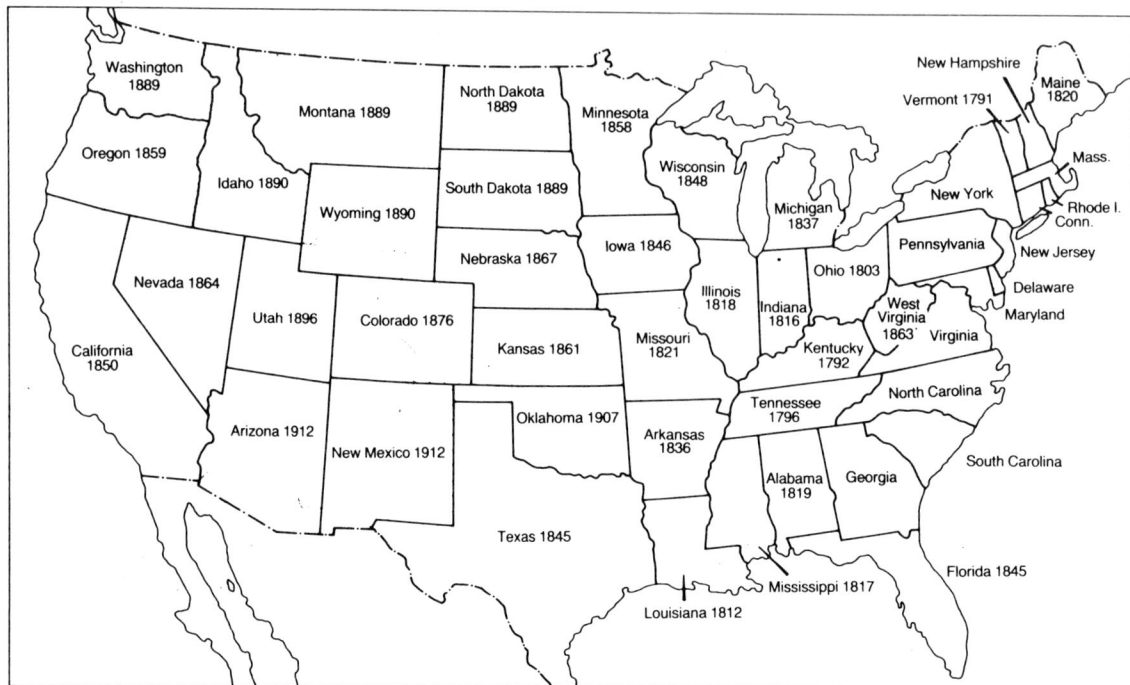

other parts of the world. The U.S.A. has been called the "melting pot" of nations, because so many migrants from every corner of the globe have gone there, settled and become Americans. But until the 1840s most of the immigrants were from north-west Europe – from England, Scotland, Ireland, Holland and Germany. The pioneer farmers who began the movement west, those who carved out towns, homesteads and communities, were, for the most part, the children and grandchildren of these early settlers, so they were, on the whole, people with similar views, beliefs and hopes, and often speaking the same language. They tended to be young, white, Anglo-Saxon and Protestant.

From the 1840s onwards the pattern of immigration began to change. Successive waves entered the United States – Irish, Germans, and, increasingly after 1880, Russians, Poles, Jews, and southern and eastern Europeans, as well as Chinese and Central Americans. The years up to the First World War saw the greatest numbers entering the States. But these people did not, on the whole, travel west; they filled the cities and factories of the East, providing a workforce that fuelled the huge growth of American capital and industry. But theirs is another story of peoples on the move.

So the people who shaped America, initially in the original 13 states and later as the West was occupied, were north-west Europeans. They laid the basis for society as a whole, believing that their way of life, their ideals of democracy and liberty, their culture and religion were the best. They feared and resented those with different faith, culture, race and colour. Irish, Chinese, Italians, Jews, Southern Blacks and Mexicans, and, later, Puerto Ricans, West Indians, Vietnamese and Central Americans, were all pushed to the bottom of the ethnic pile, tolerated as long as they stayed there, but hounded and persecuted as soon as suspicion and resentment built up.

The movement west was American and it was also male, especially during the mining bonanza, when men sometimes outnumbered women 100 to one. The diaries, letters and autobiographies of the women who went west, show that many were reluctant to give up their established homes and their families to set out for an unknown

Immigrants from Europe in the 1880s arrived at Castle Garden, New York. Here they are boarding a steamer which will take them to the Erie railway, the gateway to the cities listed on the front of the ship.

destination. For the young men, the West offered excitement and challenge, farming and hunting, but the women found they had to create a home and bring up their children in primitive and sometimes immensely lonely situations. But at the same time it was also an escape from the oppressive and often boring lives they had led in their fathers' houses in the East, where they were often denied education and prevented from finding any kind of real fulfilment. Strong feminist movements grew up in the West and were sometimes extremely successful. Wyoming, which became a state in 1890, adopted votes for women in 1869, apparently believing this might attract more people to a rather barren territory. Utah gave women the vote in 1870, again surprising for such a strongly masculine, authoritarian society, but there had arisen a fair amount of opposition from non-Mormons to Mormon dominance in the state. Giving women the vote doubled the Mormon electorate in the territory.

The movement west was American, and it was male. It was also one that stressed individual rights, where a man on his land was his own master. The communities that grew up took on this strong sense of rights, and fought fiercely to uphold law and order, but also to be allowed to carry guns, to stop Blacks voting, to ban alcohol, and a host of other issues that they saw as their right.

Elizabeth Cady Stanton:

The prejudice against color is no stronger than that against sex. . . . The Negro's skin and the woman's sex are both prima facie evidence that they were intended to be in subjection to the white Saxon man.

Ask our colored brethren if there is nothing in a name. Why are the slaves nameless unless they take that of their master? Simply because they have no independent existence. . . . Even so with women. The custom of calling women Mrs John This and Mrs Tom That, and colored men Sambo and Zip Coon, is founded on the principle that white men are the lords of all.

(Quoted in Peter N. Carroll and David W. Noble, *The Free and the Unfree; A New History of the United States*, Penguin, 1977)

The diaries and letters of migrant women often express their reluctance to uproot and journey to the unknown. Lavinia Porter left her family in Kansas in the 1860s:

I never recall that sad parting from my dear sister on the plains of Kansas without the tears flowing fast and free. . . . We were the eldest of a large family, and the bond of affection and love that existed between us was strong indeed . . . as she with the other friends turned to leave me for the ferry which was to take them back to home and civilization, I stood alone on that wild prairie. Looking westward I saw my husband driving slowly over the plain; turning my face once more to the east, my dear sister's footsteps were fast widening the distance between us. For the time I knew not which way to go, nor whom to follow. But in a few moments I rallied my forces . . . and soon overtook the slowly moving oxen who were bearing my husband and child over the green prairie . . . the unbidden tears would flow in spite of my brave resolve to be the courageous and valiant frontierswoman.

(Quoted in Jo Faragher and C. Stansell, "Women and Their Families on the Overland Trail to California and Oregon", L. Dinnerstein and K.T. Jackson, eds., *American Vistas, 1607-1877*, O.U.P., 1987)

The legacy of a pioneering society, free and independent, white and male, gun-carrying and belligerent, has its influence in the America of today. And in the English language, spoken worldwide, the echoes of the Western experience can be heard: the vocabulary of the cattlemen and cowboys – "lasso" and "lariat", "biting the dust" and "bonanza"; the vocabulary of the railroad – "side-tracked", "making the grade", "back track", "going off the rails"; the vocabulary of the saloon gamblers, "poker faced", "passing the buck", "square deal", "raw deal", "an ace up one's sleeve" and "big deal"! All this springs from an experience that was rich in excitement, danger and sheer exuberance, as well as folly and double-dealing. Some, like the Indians, were only victims; others were part of the making of a nation that dominates much of the world.

Two cities in the state of Missouri: St Louis in 1858 (above) and Kansas City in the 1960s.

Glossary

episcopalian the name given to a church, or a person belonging to that church, which is governed by bishops.

maize known in Britain as corn-on-the-cob or sweetcorn, this plant is a native of Central America and was developed by the Indians. Americans also called it Indian corn. In Britain the word "corn" is sometimes used generally for all cereal crops.

migration the general movement of people (and birds and animals) going to live in a different place. "Emigration" is the more specialized word for people leaving a country, and "immigration" for those coming into a country.

mortgage the transfer of rights in property or land in return for a loan. When the loan is paid off the mortgage is ended. If the loan cannot be paid then the property has to be given up to the one who gave the loan.

prairies or **plains** the flat treeless central grasslands of America.

range a number of meanings (for example a cooking stove and the distance a weapon will shoot or a person can see). In America, it came to be used for the open land where cattle grazed – derived from the surveying of the land in a range of strips.

reservation an area of land set aside for an Indian tribe to live on.

squatting illegally living in someone else's house or on their land.

United States of America a number of names are used for the geographical and political areas of the U.S.A., including those initials. "America" is the whole continent – South, Central and North – and North America includes Canada as well as the U.S.A., although frequently the name "America" is used to describe just the U.S.A. The nation is made up of 50 states, and is sometimes called "The States". These states form the "Union". Each state has its own government, but there is also a central government for all the states. The word "federal" is used to describe anything central, so that there are state laws and federal laws.

vigilante a citizen who voluntarily takes it upon himself to act as the law, and to capture and punish criminals.

A Note on American English
The Americans and the British both speak English, but over the years language has developed in different ways on either side of the Atlantic. There are a number of things which have different names, such as "pavement" and "sidewalk", "railways" and "railroads" and spelling often varies from one country to the other. Americans, for example, spell waggon with one "g" and leave out the "u" in "colour" and "flavour".

Date List

1783-14	United States independent from Britain.	**1843-4**	First waggons to the Pacific.
1787	North-West Territorial Ordinance.	**1844**	Mormons start trekking to Salt Lake City.
1789	George Washington becomes first President.	**1848**	Gold rush to California. U.S.-Mexican war. U.S. gains California and South-West.
1801	Thomas Jefferson becomes third President.	**1850**	California becomes a state of the Union.
1803	Louisiana Purchase.	**1850s**	"Bloody Kansas" – pro- and anti-slavery feuds.
1803-4	Lewis and Clark expedition.		
1812-14	U.S. war with Britain.	**1860s-80s**	Cattle trails.
1817-25	Building the Erie canal.	**1861-5**	U.S. Civil War. End of slavery.
1819	Treaties with Britain and Spain over western territory. First national road built across Appalachians.	**1862**	Homestead Act.
		1865	Increased immigration to U.S.A.
		1869	Transcontinental railroad completed.
1820	Missouri Compromise on slavery.	**1870s**	Indian wars.
1820s	Jedediah Smith explores the Far West.	**1876**	Battle of Little Big Horn (Custer's last stand).
1821	Mexican independence from Spain. Opening of Santa Fe Trail.	**1886**	End of the open range for cattle.
1835	Texan-Mexican war.	**1880s**	Beginnings of large-scale immigration to U.S. from south and east Europe.
1836-45	Texas an independent republic.	**1890**	End of the "Frontier". The massacre of Indians at Wounded Knee.
1838	Cherokee peoples' "Trail of Tears".		
1841	Homestead Act.		

Book List

J.M. Alvin and W. Brandon, eds, *The American Heritage Book of Indians*, New York, 1961

Richard A. Bartlett, *The New Country: A Social History of the American Frontier, 1776-1890*, Oxford University Press, 1974

*B.W. Beacroft and M.A. Smale, *The Making of America*, Longman 1982

R.A. Billington, *Westward Expansion*, New York, 1949

N.P. Hardeman, *Wilderness Calling: The Hardeman Family in the American Westward Movement, 1750-1900*, University of Tennessee Press, 1977

John A. Hawgood, *The American West*, Eyre & Spottiswoode, 1967

Pat Hodgson, *Growing Up With the North American Indians*, Batsford, 1980

Gerald W. McFarland, *A Scattered People: An American Family Moves West*, Pantheon Books, New York, 1985

*R.A. Rees and S.J. Styles, *The American West 1840-1895*, Longman, 1987

*Schools History 13-16 Project, *The American West 1840-95*, Holmes McDougall, 1977

Joseph A. Stout Jr and Odie B. Faulk, *A Short History of the American West*, Harper & Row, 1974

*Richard Tames, *Living Through History, The American West*, Batsford, 1987

*Laura Ingalls Wilder, *Little House in the Big Woods* and other titles, Puffin, 1963

* An asterisk denotes books suitable for the younger secondary school student.

Acknowledgments

The Author and Publishers would like to thank the following for permission to reproduce illustrations: Aerofilms for page 22; American Museum of Natural History for page 40; American Steel and Wire Co. for page 41 (bottom); BBC Hulton Picture Library for pages 1, 42, 46, 49, 54 and 59 (bottom); Mandel Archive for pages 5, 10, 13, 14, 20, 32, 35 (top), 36, 41 (top), 48 and 57; Mansell Collection for pages 9, 18, 21, 23, 28, 31 and 44; Mary Evans Picture Library for page 59 (top); National Film Archive, London for page 7; Nebraska State Historical Society for page 43; Smithsonian Institution National Anthropological Archives for page 15; State Historical Society of Wisconsin for page 53; US Department of Agriculture for page 55. The maps on pages 4, 12 and 56 were drawn by R.F. Brien.

Cover Illustrations
The colour print, "The Hunter's Return", is by Currier and Ives (*Mansell Collection*); the black and white print shows a railway construction crew with a wood-burning locomotive in the Cascade Mountains, 1885 (*BBC Hulton Picture Library*); the figure of the settler was drawn by Nick Theato.

Index

Numbers in italics refer to pages on which illustrations appear.

INDEX